Author's Purpose

Author's Viewpoint/Bias

Classify and Categorize

Cause and Effect

Compare and Contrast

Draw Conclusions

Fact and Opinion

Generalize

Graphic Sources

Literary Elements

Main Idea and Details

Sequence

PICTURE IT!

A Comprehension Handbook

Author's Purpose

Entertain

Inform

Persuade

Express

An author writes for many purposes including to inform, entertain, persuade, or express. An author may have more than one purpose for writing.

Classify and Categorize

When we classify and categorize, we look at how things are related based on their characteristics.

Compare and Contrast

To compare and contrast is to look for similarities and differences in things.

Draw Conclusions

When we draw conclusions, we make decisions or form an opinion about what we read.

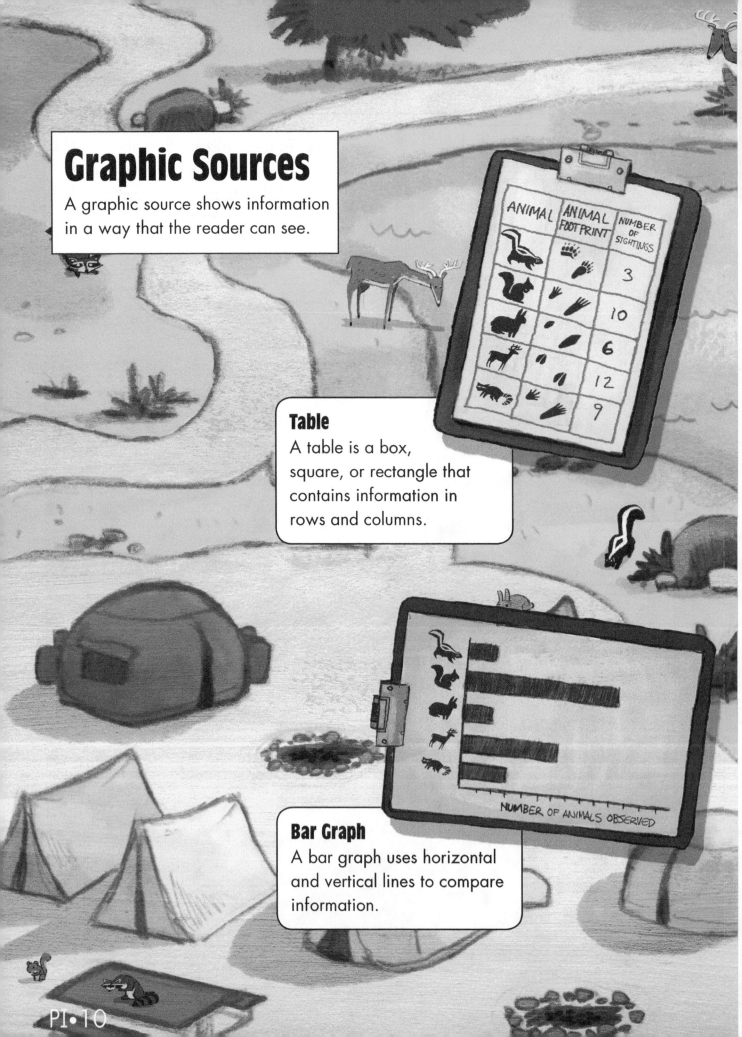

Graphic Sources

A graphic source shows information in a way that the reader can see.

ANIMAL	ANIMAL FOOTPRINT	NUMBER OF SIGHTINGS
		3
		10
		6
		12
		9

Table
A table is a box, square, or rectangle that contains information in rows and columns.

NUMBER OF ANIMALS OBSERVED

Bar Graph
A bar graph uses horizontal and vertical lines to compare information.

LAKE

N
W E
S

CAMPSITE

Map

A map is a drawing of a place and shows where something is or where something happened.

HOW TO MAKE A RAIN GAUGE.

HANGER
OR WIRE

BEND THE WIRE TO
MAKE A HOLDER AND
NAIL TO A FENCE

SCALE IN INCHES
INSIDE OF CAN

STRAIGHT-SIDED
CONTAINER FITS
IN HOLDER

Diagram

A diagram is a drawing, usually with parts that are labeled.

Literary Elements

Understanding a story requires knowing the four main parts of a story: character, setting, plot, and theme.

Setting - the time and place in which a story happens.

Character - a person or animal in a story.

Plot - the pattern of events in a story.

Climax

Rising Action

Conflict

Solution

Theme - the big idea of a story.

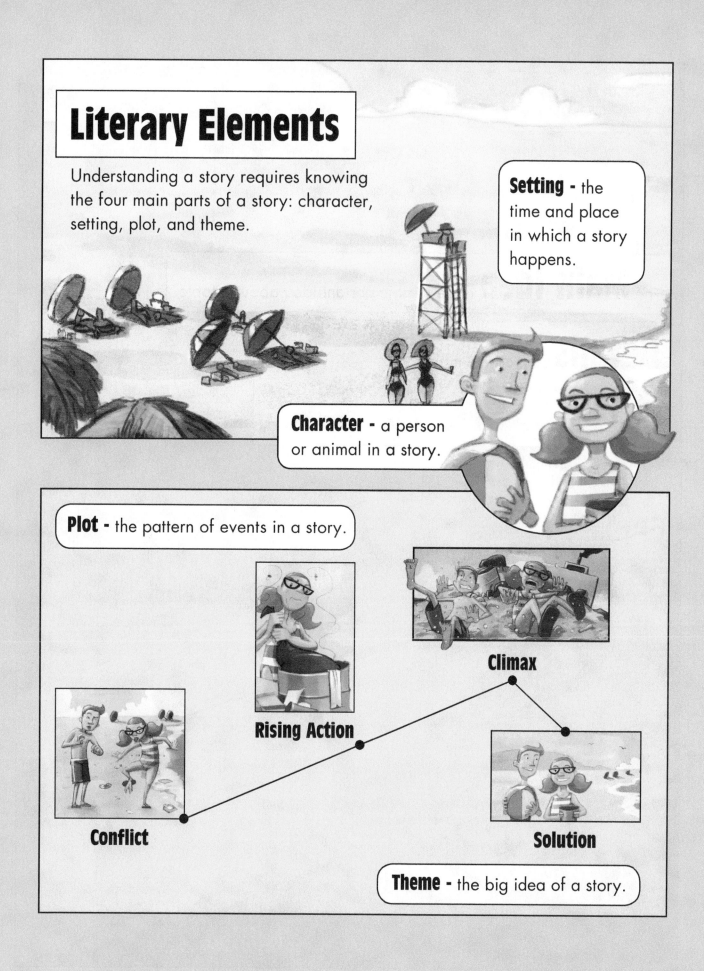

The **Main Idea** is the most important idea about a topic.

Details support the main idea.

Sequence

Sequence refers to the order of events in nonfiction.
We use sequence when we list the steps in a process.

ISBN10: 0-328-37806-2
ISBN13: 978-0-328-37806-7

9 10 11 12 13 V0UD 18 17 16 15 14
CC1

CALIFORNIA

PEARSON *LANGUAGE CENTRAL*

ELD

Consulting Authors

Jim Cummins, Ph.D.

Lily Wong Fillmore, Ph.D.

Georgia Garcia, Ph.D.

Jill Kerper Mora, Ed.D.

Glenview, Illinois • Boston, Massachusetts • Chandler, Arizona • Upper Saddle River, New Jersey

Picture It! A Comprehension Handbook   PI•1–PI•15
Words! A Vocabulary Handbook   W•1–W•14

Unit 3 Inventors and Artists

Contents

Unit 4 Adapting

Unit 5 Adventurers

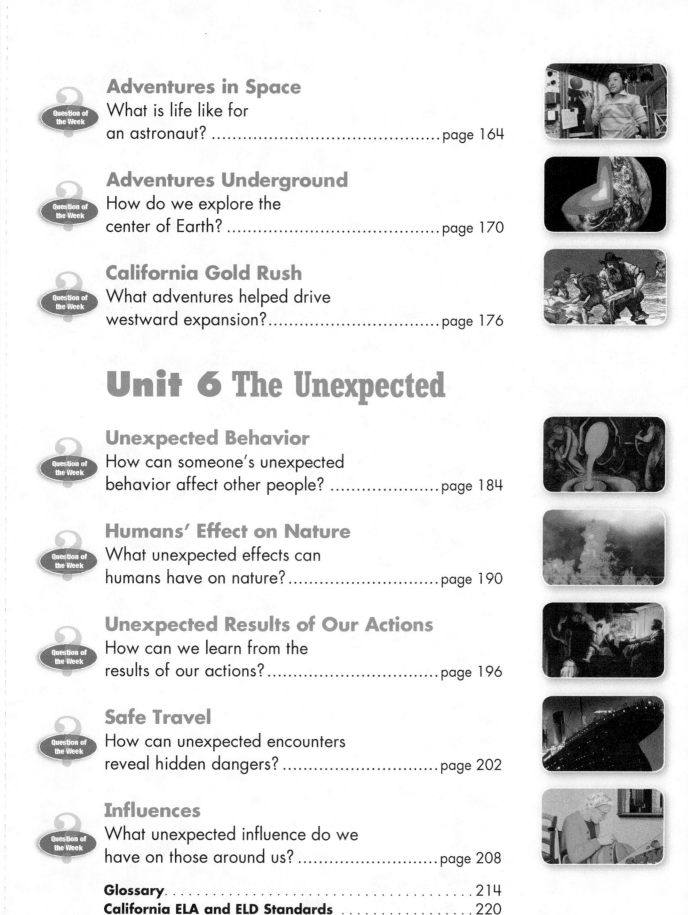

Unit 6 The Unexpected

Contents

Meeting Challenges

What kinds of challenges do people face and how do they meet them?

Courage
What inspires people to act courageously?

Challenges in Nature
How can nature challenge us?

Survival
How do people survive in the wilderness?

Personal Challenges
How do we face personal challenges?

Life in a New Country
What challenges do immigrants encounter?

Meeting Challenges

firefighter

station

brave
courageously
emergency
inspired
suddenly

What inspires people to act courageously?

Many people are inspired to act courageously in an emergency. Brave people, such as firefighters, might get scared in an emergency, but they still find courage to help others.

Read the passage together.
Then circle the vocabulary words.

A Firefighter's First Moments

Rosaria stopped at the door of Station 54 and took a deep breath. Was she ready to be a firefighter? Would she know what to do in an emergency? Could she act courageously when people needed her help?

Rosaria didn't know the answers to her questions. But she walked inside the fire station anyway. The fire trucks were shiny. The firefighters' jackets and boots were lined in a row. She saw pictures on the wall. They featured brave firefighters that had saved so many people's lives. The station was just as Rosaria had imagined.

Suddenly, Rosaria's fears went away. She felt inspired. *I can do this,* Rosaria thought. I want to help people. I am ready for any emergency!

· · · · · · · · · · · · · · · · · · · ·

Talk About It Why was Rosaria afraid? What helped her change the way she felt?

Complete the sentences below.

> Rosaria did not know if she would _____
> or if she could _____.
>
> Rosaria realized that _____.

· · · · · · · · · · · · · · · · · · · ·

Your Turn Think of a time when you were afraid but also brave. What inspired you to act courageously?

ELA R 1.3 Understand and explain frequently used synonyms, antonyms, and homographs. (ELD R EA2)

25

Describing We use words to describe people and to tell about the things they do. When we read stories, we can describe characters and tell about their actions.

We can use adjectives to describe a person. An adjective often comes before the person it describes. It can also come after the word *is* or *are*.

Example: The firefighter is **brave.**
The **brave** firefighter saved many lives.

The word *brave* tells about the firefighter in both sentences. Some other adjectives related to *brave* are *courageous*, *heroic*, and *fearless*.

We can tell what a person did by using past tense verbs. Many of these verbs end in *-ed*, such as *saved* or *climbed*.

Example: The fearless firefighter **climbed** up
the ladder toward the burning house.

Talk About It Say a sentence that describes what a brave person did. Include an adjective and a past tense verb in your sentence. Use the examples above to help you.

Your Turn Write a sentence that describes what happened in the picture. Use an adjective and a past tense verb in your sentence. Share your sentence with a partner.

_____

_____

_____

Character/Plot Most stories are about people or animals and what happens to them. The people or animals are called **characters.** What happens to the characters is called **plot.**

Adjectives can help describe the characters in a story. Past tense verbs show what characters have done. They help you talk about the plot.

Read this paragraph from a story. Circle the name of the main character.

Mrs. Carlson was walking down the street. She smelled smoke and looked around. Mrs. Carlson saw gray smoke coming from the open window of a house. Then an older man stumbled out of the house. He was coughing. Mrs. Carlson ran to the man and helped him to safety. Mrs. Carlson told the man that he would be all right. Then she called 9-1-1 using her cell phone.

Talk About It What happened in the story? What adjectives could you use to describe Mrs. Carlson based on her actions? Say a sentence that describes Mrs. Carlson.

Mrs. Carlson was _____ because she _____ .

Your Turn Complete the plot chart. Use past tense verbs to describe what happened.

Event #1: Mrs. Carlson smelled smoke.

Event #2:

Event #3:

ELA R 3.2 Identify the main problem or conflict of the plot and explain how it is resolved. (ELD R EI15)

27

Grammar

Four Kinds of Sentences There are **four kinds of sentences** in English. Each sentence ends with a different punctuation mark. The chart below shows the four kinds of sentences.

Kind of Sentence	Definition	Punctuation	Example
Declarative	It makes a statement, such as a fact or opinion.	period (.)	Scott called for help.
Interrogative	It asks a question.	question mark (?)	Is anyone hurt?
Exclamatory	It makes a statement with a lot of emotion.	exclamation point (!)	There was an accident!
Imperative	It tells someone to do something. The noun is not always written.	period (.)	Get help.

Talk About It Read each sentence and decide what kind of sentence it is. Explain your answer.

> Joe volunteered at the first-aid station.
>
> You are my hero!
>
> What would you do in an emergency?

Your Turn Imagine someone needs your help. What would you do or say? Write a sentence about the event. Tell what type of sentence it is.

_____

_____

 ELA LC 1.1 Identify and correctly use prepositional phrases, appositives, and independent and dependent clauses; use transitions and conjunctions to connect ideas. (ELD LC I7)

Think, Talk, and Write

Courage Think about how Rosaria was inspired by the pictures of brave firefighters who had saved other people's lives. Talk with a partner about what inspires you to act courageously.

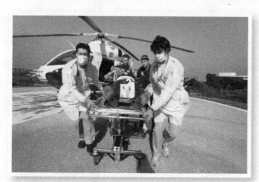

How are doctors courageous?

How are police officers courageous?

Talk About It Review the vocabulary on page 24. Work with a partner to tell about each word. Which words will you use to write about a time when you or someone you know was brave?

Produce Language Write a letter about yourself or someone you know who was courageous. First complete the chart. Then write 5 to 6 sentences in your Weekly Concept Journal.

Courageous person: _____

_____

Courageous act: _____

_____

What inspired the act: _____

_____

Vocabulary words I can use: _____

_____

ELA W 2.4 Write persuasive letters or compositions: a. State a clear position in support of a proposal. b. Support a position with relevant evidence. c. Follow a simple organizational pattern. d. Address reader concerns. (ELD W I6)

Vocabulary

PICTURE IT!

devastation

PICTURE IT!

tornado

destructive

narrow

nature

resourceful

uproot

How can nature challenge us?

Earthquakes, tornadoes, hurricanes, and monsoons are some of the ways nature challenges us. These events can cause the devastation of homes and land. People must be resourceful to survive nature's challenges.

Read the passage together.
Then circle the vocabulary words.

Tornadoes

A tornado is a powerful and destructive windstorm. A tornado spins over the land in a narrow path. The wind in a tornado can reach up to 300 miles per hour.

When and Where Tornadoes Strike

Tornadoes can strike anytime and anyplace. Most tornadoes in the United States happen in the center of the country. The tornadoes often strike during the spring and summer. Tornadoes also strike in other parts of the world.

Tornado Damage

Most tornadoes last less than 20 minutes. But they can cause terrible devastation and loss of life. Tornadoes can flip cars, uproot trees, and destroy buildings.

. . . .

Talk About It What makes tornadoes so dangerous? Complete the sentences below.

> A tornado has winds _____ and can _____ .
>
> A tornado can strike _____ and can
>
> cause _____ .

. . . .

Your Turn Think of a storm you can remember. What was the storm like? What did you do during the storm? Tell a partner about the storm.

Cause and Effect Relationship We use words to tell why things happen. Sometimes a word or phrase is used to connect what happened and why it happened.

An example with cause and effect words is shown below.

A tornado struck the town.
As a result, trees were uprooted.

Circle the word or phrase in each example that connects two events.

because	The road is empty because a storm is on its way.
therefore	The tornado was very strong. Therefore, the destruction was terrible.
for this reason, as a result	The storm came closer. For this reason, the sky grew darker.

Talk About It Say one or two sentences about a storm you saw. Use a cause and effect word or phrase to explain what happened.

Your Turn Write a sentence that tells what is happening in this picture. Include a cause and effect word or phrase in your sentence.

_____

_____

_____

Cause and Effect When we read, we learn about events and why they happen. A **cause** makes an **effect** happen. When you read, look for words and phrases that show cause and effect. To find a cause, ask yourself, "Why did this happen?" To find an effect, ask yourself, "What happened?"

Cause and Effect	
Cause	Effects
A tornado strikes a city. ➡	_____ _____

Write two effects of a tornado striking a town in the chart above.

Talk About It Look at the picture of the house after a tornado. What do you think happened? Complete the sentences below with a partner.

As a result of the tornado, _____.

The house _____ because of the tornado.

Your Turn Look at the passage on page 31 about tornadoes. What effects can a tornado cause?

_____

_____

_____

ELA G4 R 2.6 Distinguish between cause and effect and between fact and opinion in expository text. (ELD R EA16)

33

Grammar

Subjects and Predicates English sentences have two parts. The first part is the **subject.** The subject shows who or what the sentence is about. The second part is the **predicate.** The predicate tells us something about the subject. The chart below splits sentences by subject and predicate.

Subject	Predicate
The tornadoes	strike the town.
Streets	flood.
Cristina and Jenny	help clean up.

Talk About It Read the sentences. Circle the subjects. Underline the predicates.

> The storm caused a lot of damage.
>
> Luis and Claudia talked about the tornado.

Your Turn Finish these sentences. Choose a subject or predicate from the box. Then write a new sentence of your own. Circle the subject. Underline the predicate.

Mr. Thomas	Teresa and Jim	gathers supplies

The family _____.

_____ calls the neighbors.

_____ head to the basement.

_____

_____

 ELA LC 1.1 Identify and correctly use prepositional phrases, appositives, and independent and dependent clauses; use transitions and conjunctions to connect ideas. (ELD LC I7)

Think, Talk, and Write

Challenges in Nature Think about how nature challenges people. Talk with a partner about how people can work together after a natural disaster.

How do people rebuild?

How do volunteers help?

- -

Talk About It Review the vocabulary on page 30. Work with a partner to tell about each word. Which words will you use to write about ways that people can survive nature's challenges?

- -

Produce Language Write about one way that people can survive nature's challenges. First complete the chart. Then write 5 to 6 sentences in your Weekly Concept Journal.

Nature's challenge: _____

_____

What can happen: _____

_____

How people can help each other: _____

_____

Vocabulary words I can use: _____

_____

ELA W 2.1 Write narratives: a. Establish a plot, point of view, setting, and conflict. b. Show, rather than tell, the events of the story. (ELD W I1)

35

Vocabulary

campfire

ravine

trail

wilderness

camped

gnawed

plenty

survive

How do people survive in the wilderness?

It is not easy to survive in the wilderness, but people have learned how. They find ways to get food and water. They also find ways to keep warm.

Vocabulary in Context

Read the passage together.
Then circle the vocabulary words.

Life on the Trail

Eli's Journal

May 15, 1850

My family and I are getting closer to Oregon! We have been traveling on the Oregon Trail for one month. Last night we camped near a ravine. The first thing we did was look for water. My sisters and I found some water in the ravine and filled three jugs. Then Father made a campfire. Mother was upset because a squirrel gnawed through a bag of flour. Luckily, there was plenty left. We mixed flour and water together to make bread. Working together made things easier. I was so tired, though, I fell asleep soon after I finished eating my dinner!

. . . .

Talk About It What did Eli's family do to survive in the wilderness? Complete the sentences below.

Eli and his sisters _____ so they could _____.

Working together _____.

. . . .

Your Turn How would you survive in the wilderness? Share your ideas with a partner. Then discuss which ideas you think are best.

ELA LS 1.2 Interpret a speaker's verbal and nonverbal messages, purposes, and perspectives. (ELD LS I2)

37

Language Workshop

FORM & FUNCTION

Literary Analysis We use words to discuss stories we read. We can talk about the setting, or where and when a story takes place. Special words help show where and when the story takes place.

Example: The story takes place **on** the beach **at** night **in** the wilderness.

Circle the words that tell where and when.

Where	**When**
on the beach	at night
in the wilderness	after sunset
by a campfire	in the present
near the water	during the summer

Talk About It Look at the picture. Use the picture to think of a setting for a story. Use words that tell both where and when.

Complete the sentence.

The story takes place at _____ on _____ .

Your Turn Look at the picture above. Use the picture to write a sentence about the setting of a story. Use words that tell both where and when.

_____

_____

_____

 ELA W 1.1 Create multiple-paragraph narrative compositions: a. Establish and develop a situation or plot. b. Describe the setting. c. Present an ending. (ELD W I5)

Theme/Setting A story's **setting** can be real or made up. For example, the setting of the story "Life on the Trail" on page 37 is during a real time and place in history. The setting can influence the theme of the story. The **theme** is the main message or big idea of a story. The theme of "Life on the Trail" is that in difficult situations, working together makes things easier.

Talk About It Reread "Life on the Trail" on page 37. What is the setting? What details help you imagine the setting? Why is the setting a good choice for expressing the theme of the story?

Complete the sentences with a partner. Use words that tell where and when to describe the setting.

> The story takes place in _____ on _____.
>
> Because the story was set in the wilderness, it helped show how important it is for people _____.

Your Turn Think of another setting for a story in which people must survive in the wilderness. Describe the setting here.

_____

_____

_____

_____

_____

_____

_____

 **ELA R 3.1** Identify and analyze the characteristics of poetry, drama, fiction, and nonfiction and explain the appropriateness of the literary forms chosen by an author for a specific purpose. **ELA R 3.4** Understand that *theme* refers to the meaning or moral of a selection and recognize themes (whether implied or stated directly) in sample works. (ELD W EA3)

Independent and Dependent Clauses A clause is a group of words that has a subject and a predicate. An **independent clause** is a complete thought that can stand alone. It is a complete sentence. A **dependent clause** is not a complete thought and cannot stand alone. A dependent clause needs to be paired with an independent clause in a sentence.

Type of Clause	Complete thought?	Example
Independent	yes	Jake bought a map.
Dependent	no	because Jake wants to go on a hike
Independent + Dependent	yes	Jake bought a map because he wants to go on a hike.

Talk About It Read the sentences below. Circle the sentences that are complete thoughts.

The friends looked at the map.

The friends went on a hike.

Because they were lost.

Your Turn Find the incomplete thought above. Add words to make the dependent clause a complete thought.

Write the new sentence below.

_____

_____

 ELA LC 1.1 Identify and correctly use prepositional phrases, appositives, and independent and dependent clauses; use transitions and conjunctions to connect ideas. (ELD LC EA7)

Think, Talk, and Write

Survival Think about the ways Eli's family worked together to survive in 1850. Talk with a partner about how surviving in the wilderness is different today.

How do we keep food safe?

How do we travel quickly?

Talk About It Review the vocabulary on page 36. Work with a partner to tell about each word. Which words will you use to write about how to survive in the wilderness?

Produce Language Write a story that shows how people can survive in the wilderness. First complete the chart. Then write 5 to 6 sentences in your Weekly Concept Journal.

My characters: _____

_____

Wilderness setting: _____

_____

How they survive: _____

_____

Vocabulary words I can use: _____

_____

ELA W 2.1 Write narratives: a. Establish a plot, point of view, setting, and conflict. b. Show, rather than tell, the events of the story. (ELD W I3)

41

Vocabulary

competition

gymnast

confidence
intellectual
overcome
personal
physical
unique

How do we face personal challenges?

Everyone faces personal challenges. These challenges might be physical, such as being sick. They might be intellectual, such as learning to read. People work to overcome challenges.

Vocabulary in Context

Read the passage together.
Then circle the vocabulary words.

Meet A Special Olympian

"Let me win. But if I cannot win, let me be brave in the attempt." —from the Special Olympics Oath

Special Olympics is a unique program for people with intellectual disabilities. Special Olympics helps these athletes play sports. The Special Olympics World Games is an important physical competition. It has many events.

Monica Rivas is a gymnast, like the girl in the picture. Monica grew up in El Salvador. Rivas had personal challenges. Learning was hard for her. She used sign language to talk to people. She was very shy.

Rivas joined Special Olympics when she was nine. Then she began to train and compete. Special Olympics helped Rivas gain confidence. No challenge held her back anymore. Now Rivas helps other people in El Salvador get involved in Special Olympics.

- -

Talk About It Why is Special Olympics unique and important? Complete the sentences below.

> Special Olympics helps give people _____ .
>
> Special Olympics athletes _____ in many sports.

- -

Your Turn What challenges did Monica Rivas overcome? How did she do it? Tell a partner.

ELA R 1.4 Know abstract, derived roots and affixes from Greek and Latin and use this knowledge to analyze the meaning of complex words (e.g., *controversial*). (ELD R I6)

43

Sequencing Sequence is the order in which things happen. We can use certain words to help show sequence.

Example: **First,** the runner did not have confidence. But **then,** he decided to work harder. **After** much hard work, he **finally** got faster.

Circle the words that show sequence in the sentences below.

before, now	Before, the runner was afraid, but now he is confident.
after, afterward	We watched my brother compete, and afterward we had a picnic.
first, second, next, then	The swimming relay races come next.
last, finally	Finally, the winners received medals.

Talk About It Say a sentence that tells how you or someone you know overcame a personal challenge. Use sequence words from the chart.

Your Turn Write about overcoming a personal challenge. Use at least two sequence words.

_____

_____

_____

Comprehension Support

Sequence When we read a story, it is easier to understand when we know the order in which things happened. By understanding **sequence,** we can see how a character changed over time. This helps us see what the character accomplished and why his or her life is important. When you read, look for clue words that help show sequence.

Read the sentences below, and circle the sequence words.

First, Reggie could not play basketball. Then, Reggie practiced running, jumping, and throwing. Now, Reggie is on the basketball team.

· ·

Talk About It Tell how Reggie changed. Use sequence words. Complete the sentences below with a partner.

> First, Reggie _____ . Then, Reggie _____ .
>
> Now, Reggie _____ .

· ·

Your Turn Circle the sequence word in each sentence. Then read the sentences in the correct order. Use the sequence words to help you determine when things happened.

Then, Reggie practiced running, jumping, and throwing.

First, Reggie could not play basketball.

Now, Reggie is on the basketball team.

Grammar

Compound and Complex Sentences Some sentences have more than one independent clause, which is a complete thought. A **compound sentence** is made up of two or more independent clauses. A **complex sentence** is made up of at least one independent clause and at least one dependent clause. Special words connect the clauses.

	Compound Sentence	**Complex Sentence**
Definition:	two or more independent clauses	one or more independent clauses AND one or more dependent clauses
Needs:	clauses connected by a comma and often one of these words: **and, but, or, so**	comma after the dependent clause IF the clause is at the beginning of a sentence
Example:	Ivan could not swim, **so** Carlos helped him learn.	**Because** Ivan could not swim, Carlos helped him learn.

Talk About It Read the sentences. Decide whether each sentence is compound or complex.

> When Jane practiced, she became a good soccer player.
>
> The skateboard was old, but Jamal liked to ride it.

Your Turn Finish each sentence. Then tell whether the sentence is compound or complex.

After Jesse won the race, _____

_____.

Kim wanted to help Rita, _____

_____.

ELA G6 LC 1.1 Use simple, compound, and compound-complex sentences; use effective coordination and subordination of ideas to express complete thoughts. (ELD G6 LC EI11)

Think, Talk, and Write

Personal Challenges Think about how Monica Rivas overcame her challenges to compete as a gymnast. Talk with a partner about a time when you overcame a personal challenge.

Is learning math
a challenge?

Is learning to play the
piano a challenge?

- -

Talk About It Review the vocabulary on page 42. Work with a partner to tell about each word. Which words will you use to write about a time when you overcame a personal challenge?

- -

Produce Language Write about a time when you overcame a personal challenge. First complete the chart. Then write 5 to 6 sentences in your Weekly Concept Journal.

My challenge: _____
_____

Why it was a challenge: _____
_____

How I overcame my challenge: _____
_____

Vocabulary words I can use: _____
_____

ELA W 2.1 Write narratives: a. Establish a plot, point of view, setting, and conflict. b. Show, rather than tell, the events of the story. (ELD W I3)

47

Life in a New Country

baggage

island

encounter
immigrants
legal
previous
quicker
seeking

What challenges do immigrants encounter?

It is not easy to move from one country to another. Immigrants need to find jobs and learn about laws. Often, immigrants must learn a new language. Millions of immigrants have come to the United States.

Read the passage together.
Then circle the vocabulary words.

Ellis Island

Ellis Island is an island near New York City. It is an important part of American history. More than 12 million people arrived at Ellis Island between 1892 and 1954. The immigrants came from many different countries. Imagine the different languages spoken at Ellis Island. When immigrants arrived, workers would inspect their legal papers. Doctors also examined immigrants to check whether they were healthy.

Immigrants came to the United States seeking a better life. Many immigrants may have missed their previous countries. Perhaps they filled their baggage with pictures to remember the past. Other immigrants were probably quicker to forget their previous homes. But all immigrants would encounter challenges.

Talk About It What do you know about immigrants and Ellis Island? Complete the sentences below.

> Immigrants _____ Ellis Island for many years.
>
> Immigrants were different from one another because _____.
>
> Immigrants were like one another because _____.

Your Turn What are some challenges you might encounter when moving to a new country? Tell a partner.

Cause and Effect Relationship We can show cause and effect by using the words *if* and *then*. The words after *if* tell a possible cause. The words after *then* tell a possible effect.

Example: **If** they move to Mexico, **then** they (will learn) Spanish.

The verb *will learn* is circled in the sentence above. The verb *will learn* is in the future tense. Notice that the word *move* is in the present tense. This is the pattern in most *if/then* sentences.

Circle the words *if* and *then*. Underline the verbs.

> If we live near the ocean, then I will swim every day.
>
> If my new school is far away, then I will ride the bus.
>
> If we stay in Mexico, then I will miss my old friends.

Talk About It Say an *if/then* sentence about immigrants.
Use the examples above to help you with the sentence pattern.

Your Turn Write an *if/then* sentence about immigrants.
Remember to put a comma before the word *then*.

_____

_____

ELA LC 1.1 Identify and correctly use prepositional phrases, appositives, and independent and dependent clauses; use transitions and conjunctions to connect ideas. (ELD LC I8)

Cause and Effect Many articles and stories tell what happens and why it happens. This is called **cause and effect.** A cause is why something happens. An effect is what happens.

Clue words and phrases, such as *because, so that, as a result, for this reason,* and *therefore* can show cause and effect. *If/then* sentences can also show cause and effect. Sometimes there are no clue words.

Circle the clue words that show cause and effect below.

People came to the United States so that they could have a better life.

Some immigrants were sad because they missed their old homes.

Talk About It Look at the picture. What is happening?

Complete the sentences below with a partner.

Marcos and his mother are unpacking because _____.

Marcos is being careful so that _____.

If Marcos breaks a dish, then _____.

Your Turn Imagine you are moving to a new city or country. Write a sentence about moving that shows cause and effect. Use clue words in your sentence.

_____

_____

ELA R 2.3 Discern main ideas and concepts presented in texts, identifying and assessing evidence that supports those ideas. (ELD R I14)

51

Common and Proper Nouns A **proper noun** names a specific person, place, or thing. A proper noun begins with a capital letter. A **common noun** names a nonspecific person, place, or thing. It begins with a lowercase letter. The chart below gives examples of common and proper nouns.

	Common	Proper	Examples
person	boy	José	That boy, José, moved to a new city.
place	state	California	California, a state in this country, is large.
thing	store	Star Hardware	Star Hardware, a nearby store, is open.

Talk About It Read the sentences with a partner. Circle the common nouns. Underline the proper nouns. Who is the teacher in the second sentence?

Mr. Adams moved to California for a new job.

Ms. Smith, a teacher, is going to visit her old country, England.

Your Turn Finish the sentences. Use a mix of common nouns and proper nouns.

Marie, _____, moved from France to _____.

Marie will go to a new school called _____.

At her new school, Marie will learn _____.

ELA LC 1.4 Use correct capitalization. (ELD LC I8)

Think, Talk, and Write

Life in a New Country Think about the Ellis Island immigrants long ago. How is living in a new country different today than it was in the early 1900s?

How do people
learn a new language?

How do people find jobs?

Talk About It Review the vocabulary on page 48. Work with a partner to tell about each word. Which words will you use to write to a new immigrant about life in the United States?

Produce Language Write a letter to a new immigrant about what is challenging and what is great about living in the United States. First complete the chart. Then write 5 to 6 sentences in your Weekly Concept Journal.

What I like the most: _____
_____

Why I like it: _____
_____

What is challenging: _____
_____

Vocabulary words I can use: _____
_____

ELA W 2.4 Write persuasive letters or compositions: a. State a clear position in support of a proposal. b. Support a position with relevant evidence. c. Follow a simple organizational pattern. d. Address reader concerns. (ELD W EA5)

53

Doing the
Right Thing

THE BIG ?

What makes
people want to
do the right thing?

Honesty
Why is honesty important?

Taking Risks
Why do we help others even if there are risks?

Helping Others
What are the rewards in helping others?

Protecting Animals
What can people do to protect wild animals?

Promoting Freedom
How can people promote freedom?

Doing the Right Thing

Honesty

Vocabulary

PICTURE IT!

driftwood

PICTURE IT!

hammocks

concealed
honest
sternly
truth

Why is honesty important?

It is important to be honest so people will trust you. Honest people refuse to lie, cheat, or steal. An honest person can be counted on to do the right thing.

Vocabulary in Context

Read the passage together.
Then circle the vocabulary words.

A Day at the Beach

Paula, Molly, and their younger cousin Joshua raced down the beach toward the hammocks, leaping over pieces of driftwood. They noticed a man walking away.

Joshua saw a black wallet in the sand. "Look! That man dropped his wallet." He opened it and whooped, "Forty dollars!" He concealed the wallet in his pocket.

"Joshua!" Molly said sternly. "That's wrong!"

"You have to be honest," said Paula. "Good things happen when we tell the truth."

"Hi, kids," a voice said. The man had returned. "Have you seen a wallet anywhere? I've lost mine."

Joshua looked at his cousins and said, "Here it is!"

After saying thank you, the man introduced himself. Joshua's mouth dropped open. He had just met the author of his favorite book!

· ·

Talk About It Why is it important to be honest? Tell a partner. Use the sentence frames below.

> It is important to be honest because _____.
>
> When you are honest, sometimes _____.

· ·

Your Turn Why do you think Joshua returned the wallet? Tell a partner.

ELA R 1.1 Read aloud narrative and expository text fluently and accurately and with appropriate pacing, intonation, and expression. (ELD R EA1)

57

Language Workshop FORM & FUNCTION

Comparing and Contrasting We use words to tell how things or people are similar and how they are different. When we compare, we tell how things are similar. When we contrast, we tell how things are different.

Example: **Both** Molly and Paula were **more honest than** Joshua in the beginning of the story.

We can use special words and sentence patterns to show similarities and differences between the things or people we are comparing and contrasting.

Circle the words that show similarities and differences in the sentences below.

more, than	Honest people are more respected than dishonest people.
-er words	Both Molly and Paula were wiser than Joshua. Molly and Paula are older than Joshua.
-est words	Of all the friends, Joshua was the saddest because he didn't feel like anyone trusted him.
most	Compared to Molly and Paula, Joshua was the most dishonest.

Talk About It Say a sentence that compares or contrasts honest people with dishonest people. Use the examples above to help you.

Your Turn Look at the picture of this group of friends. Write one sentence that tells how the friends are similar. Write another sentence that tells how the friends are different. Use two words from the chart above.

_____

_____

ELA LC 1.1 Identify and correctly use prepositional phrases, appositives, and independent and dependent clauses; use transitions and conjunctions to connect ideas. (ELD LC I8)

Compare and Contrast As we read, it is important to **compare and contrast.** *Both*, *like*, and *as* are clue words that show comparisons. *Unlike* and *but* are clue words that show contrasts. Words that end with *-er* and *-est* also signal that a contrast is being made.

Read the paragraph together. Circle clue words that show comparisons and contrasts.

Both Confucius and Abraham Lincoln were honest leaders. Confucius lived in ancient China, but Abraham Lincoln lived in the United States. Lincoln, like Confucius, knew honesty was better than dishonesty. Some believe that Lincoln's reputation for honesty helped him be elected President of the United States. Confucius was once forced out of China. His reputation as an honest person helped him, though, and he was allowed to return home.

Talk About It Look at the paragraph above. Compare and contrast Lincoln and Confucius. Complete the sentences below with a partner.

> Both Lincoln and Confucius _____.
>
> Unlike Confucius, Lincoln _____.

Your Turn Write a sentence that compares or contrasts Lincoln and Confucius. Use *like*, *both*, or *unlike* in your sentence.

_____

_____

ELA G4 R 2.1 Identify structural patterns found in informational text (e.g., compare and contrast, cause and effect, sequential or chronological order, proposition and support) to strengthen comprehension. (ELD R EA11)

59

Grammar

Regular and Irregular Nouns Nouns name people, places, and things. A plural noun names more than one of something. Plural nouns can be **regular** or **irregular.** A regular plural noun is formed by adding -s or -es to the end of the noun. Irregular plural nouns do not follow this rule.

Regular Nouns	Irregular Nouns
What is your greatest **talent?** Confucius used his **talents** wisely.	A **person** should try to be honest. Many **people** live honestly.
Confucius was a good **friend.** Honest people have many **friends.**	The **life** of Confucius is well known. Confucius enriched the **lives** of others.
I didn't take your **glass!** More **glasses** are in the cabinet.	The **child** always told the truth. All the **children** played fairly together.

Talk About It Read the sentences and circle the plural nouns.

The two women found the wallet.
They gave it to the store clerk.

Heroes are fun to learn about.

Your Turn Finish the sentence below using a plural noun from the chart. Then write your own sentence using a regular or irregular noun from the chart.

A lot of _____ value honesty.

_____

_____

 ELA LC 1.5 Spell roots, suffixes, prefixes, contractions, and syllable constructions correctly. (ELD LC I8)

Honesty Think about how telling the truth can lead to good things happening. Talk with a partner about why honesty is important.

Why is honesty important for businesses?

Why is honesty important in sports?

Talk About It Review the vocabulary on page 56. Work with a partner to tell about each word. Which words will you use to write about honesty?

Produce Language Write about why honesty is important at home, at work, or at school. First complete the chart. Then write 5 to 6 sentences in your Weekly Concept Journal.

Place where honesty is important: _____

_____

Why honesty is important: _____

_____

What happens if people are not honest: _____

_____

Vocabulary words I can use: _____

_____

ELA W 2.3 Write research reports about important ideas, issues, or events by using the following guidelines: a. Frame questions that direct the investigation. b. Establish a controlling idea or topic. c. Develop the topic with simple facts, details, examples, and explanations. (ELD W I4)

Vocabulary

PICTURE IT!

collapsed

PICTURE IT!

rescue

heroine

moral

representatives

risks

superiors

Why do we help others even if there are risks?

Most people are moral. Moral people have beliefs that guide them to do the right thing. They enjoy helping others. Some people, such as Kate Shelley, help others even when there are risks.

Read the passage together.
Then circle the vocabulary words.

Saving the Midnight Express

On July 6, 1881, fifteen-year-old Kate Shelley became a heroine. A local train engine was checking the railroad tracks during a storm. When it crossed the bridge near Kate's house, the bridge collapsed.

The Midnight Express passenger train would be crossing that bridge. Kate knew that it needed to be warned. People would die if the train tried to cross the bridge. Kate crossed another bridge and rushed into the station. She warned the railroad representatives about the collapsed bridge.

The railroad representatives called their superiors, who stopped the Express train in time. Kate and the representatives then went to rescue the two crewmen who were in the train engine when the bridge collapsed.

Talk About It How did Kate Shelley become a heroine? Complete the sentences below.

> Kate Shelley took a risk and saved _____ from crashing.
>
> She helped rescue _____.

Your Turn Think about Kate Shelley's heroism. What would you have done if you had been there? Tell a partner what you would have done.

 ELA R 1.1 Read aloud narrative and expository text fluently and accurately and with appropriate pacing, intonation, and expression. (ELD R EA1)

Language Workshop

 FORM & FUNCTION

Retelling When we tell a story about a person's life or an event, we tell what happened first. Then, we describe what happened next. We also tell how and when the event happened.

We use phrases that tell when and past tense verbs to retell events.

Example: The train **started** to cross the bridge.
At that moment, the bridge collapsed.

In the sentences below, circle the phrases that tell when and the past tense verbs that tell what happened.

When	What	Sentences
during	**broke**	During the storm, the bridge broke into pieces.
at that moment	**fell**	At that moment, the train fell into the river.
on July 6, 1881	**crossed**	On July 6, 1881, Kate crossed a bridge over the Des Moines River.
within minutes	**tossed**	Within minutes, the rescue team tossed the engineer a rope.

Talk About It Retell what happened to the bridge. Use the words above to help guide you.

• •

Your Turn Write a sentence that retells what Kate Shelley did. Use words that tell what happened and when.

_____

_____

_____

ELA LS 2.3 Deliver oral responses to literature: a. Summarize significant events and details. b. Articulate an understanding of several ideas or images communicated by the literary work. c. Use examples of textual evidence from the work to support conclusions. (ELD LS I5)

Comprehension Support

Author's Purpose Authors write to persuade, to inform, to entertain, or to express. Sometimes there is more than one **author's purpose.** When authors write about a person's life, they use past tense verbs to retell what that person did.

Read the paragraph below. The author is writing to inform readers of Kate Shelley's actions. The author also is writing to persuade readers that kids can make a difference.

It is important to assist others when they need help. Kate Shelley was a heroine at the age of fifteen. She crossed a slippery bridge during a major storm. She ran quickly to the train station. She warned the railroad representatives that the bridge had collapsed, which saved the Midnight Express. She proved that kids can make a difference too!

Talk About It Look at the paragraph above. What does the author say to persuade you that kids can make a difference?

Complete the sentences below with a partner.

Kate Shelley helped save a train when she was only _____.

She crossed a _____ and she _____.

Your Turn Write a sentence to show your reader what kids have done to help others. Use a past tense verb.

_____

_____

ELA R 3.1 Identify and analyze the characteristics of poetry, drama, fiction, and nonfiction and explain the appropriateness of the literary forms chosen by an author for a specific purpose. (ELD R I12)

65

Grammar

Possessive Nouns A noun that shows possession, or ownership, is called a **possessive noun.** Possessive nouns are made by adding an apostrophe and -s or only an apostrophe. In the first column of the chart below, the noun is in bold. In the second column, the sentence has been rewritten to make the noun possessive.

Noun	Possessive Noun
Kate used a lantern to light her way.	That is **Kate's** lantern.
The **train** was due soon.	A collapsed bridge was in the **train's** path.
The railroad **representatives** hurried to save the **people** on the train.	The **representatives'** actions saved **people's** lives.

Talk About It Read the sentences and circle the possessive nouns.

The creek's water was choppy from the storm.

The train's headlight is on.

Your Turn Finish these sentences. Use possessive nouns from the chart. Then use a possessive noun to write a sentence of your own.

Was the _____ crew saved?

How could the _____ actions save the train?

_____

_____

ELA LC 1.2 Identify and correctly use verbs that are often misused (e.g., *lie/lay, sit/set, rise/raise*), modifiers, and pronouns. (ELD LC I8)

Think, Talk, and Write

Taking Risks Think about how Kate Shelley saved passengers on the train. Talk with a partner about why people take risks to help others.

Why do people take risks to save people in danger?

How do people take risks for each other?

Talk About It Review the vocabulary on page 62. Work with a partner to tell about each word. Which words will you use to write about someone you know who took a risk to help others?

Produce Language Write about someone you know who took a risk to help others. First complete the chart. Then write 5 to 6 sentences in your Weekly Concept Journal.

My hero: _____

_____

My hero's risk: _____

_____

Why he or she helped: _____

_____

Vocabulary words I can use: _____

_____

ELA W 2.1 Write narratives: a. Establish a plot, point of view, setting, and conflict. b. Show, rather than tell, the events of the story. (ELD W I3)

67

Vocabulary

PICTURE IT!

cloak

PICTURE IT!

seamstress

appreciation
assistance
astonished
gratitude
possession

What are the rewards in helping others?

Helping others when they need assistance can make you feel good about yourself. It may also help you. Sometimes a person we help one day will help us out another day.

Vocabulary in Context

Read the passage together.
Then circle the vocabulary words.

A Drum:
An Indian Folk Tale

A boy wished for a drum to play, but he had no money. All he had was a piece of bread.

Along the road, the boy saw a young seamstress. She was thin and crying. The boy knew the seamstress was much hungrier than he was, so he gave her his bread. With gratitude, the seamstress gave him a coat she had made. It was her favorite possession.

The boy then saw a traveling musician. He was very cold because robbers had stolen his cloak. The boy gave the musician his coat. In appreciation, the astonished man then gave the boy his drum.

. . . .

Talk About It Why did the seamstress and the musician want to show their gratitude to the boy? Complete the sentences below with a partner.

The seamstress was _____, and the boy gave her _____.

Both the seamstress and the musician appreciated the boy's _____.

. . . .

Your Turn Think about a time when you helped someone. Tell a partner about it.

ELA R 1.1 Read aloud narrative and expository text fluently and accurately and with appropriate pacing, intonation, and expression. (ELD R I2)

69

Language Workshop FORM& FUNCTION

Comparing and Contrasting We can use words to tell how things are alike and different. When we compare, we tell how things are alike, or similar. When we contrast, we tell how things are different.

Example: The seamstress was **much hungrier** than the boy.

Circle the words that show similarities and differences in the sentences below.

both	Both the seamstress and the musician were grateful.
like	Like the seamstress, the musician was grateful.
unlike	Unlike the boy, the seamstress had no food to eat.
while	The boy ended up with a drum, while the musician ended up with a cloak.
much + -er word	The boy was much happier after he had helped the others.

Talk About It Look at these two groups of students helping in the pictures. Say one sentence that compares and one sentence that contrasts how these students are helping. Use words that show similarities and differences.

Your Turn Write a sentence that compares or contrasts how the students are helping. Use a word that shows similarities or differences in your sentence.

_____

_____

_____

 ELA LC 1.1 Identify and correctly use prepositional phrases, appositives, and independent and dependent clauses; use transitions and conjunctions to connect ideas. (ELD LC I8)

Compare and Contrast When we read, it is important to **compare** and **contrast.** *Both, like,* and *as* are clue words that show comparisons. *Unlike, while,* and *but* are clue words that show contrasts.

Circle the clue words that show comparisons and contrasts below.

Sara and Juan both wanted to help others. Sara wanted to work with young children, while Juan was thinking about working at an animal shelter. Juan thought that he would be good at helping care for dogs and cats. Unlike Juan, Sara thought that she would be much better at planning fun activities for kids.

Talk About It How are Juan and Sara similar? How are they different? Complete the sentences below with a partner.

Like Sara, Juan _____.

Unlike Juan, Sara _____.

Your Turn Use the graphic organizer to compare and contrast Sara and Juan. Write how they are similar and different.

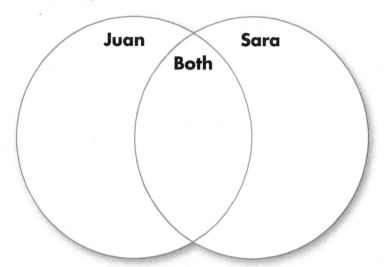

Juan **Both** **Sara**

ELA G4 R 2.1 Identify structural patterns found in informational text (e.g., compare and contrast, cause and effect, sequential or chronological order, proposition and support) to strengthen comprehension. (ELD R EA16)

71

Action Verbs An **action verb** shows someone doing something.
Some action verbs show actions you can see, such as *run* and *jump.*
Some action verbs show actions you can't see, such as *think* or *hope.*
Examples of action verbs are circled in the chart below.

Action Verbs You Can See	Action Verbs You Can't See
The boy (walked) down the street.	The boy (hoped) he would get a drum.
The thieves (stole) the musician's cloak.	The musician (thought) the boy was helpful.
The seamstress (gave) the boy a coat.	The seamstress (worried) that nobody would help her.

Talk About It Read the sentences and circle the action verbs.

> The lion struggled against the net.
>
> The mouse ran through the lion's den.

Your Turn Finish the sentences below. Use action verbs from the chart. Then study the photograph. Use an action verb to write a sentence of your own about the boy.

The boy _____ about what he could do.

The boy _____ the musician a coat.

_____

_____

_____

 ELA LC 1.2 Identify and correctly use verbs that are often misused (e.g., *lie/lay, sit/set, rise/raise*), modifiers, and pronouns. (ELD LC I7)

Think, Talk, and Write

Helping Others Think about how the boy was rewarded for his kindness to the seamstress and the musician. Talk with a partner about other ways children can help others.

How can children help make people happy?

How can children help feed people?

Talk About It Review the vocabulary on page 68. Work with a partner to tell about each word. Which words will you use to write about a time when you helped others?

Produce Language Write about a time you helped others. First complete the chart. Then write 5 to 6 sentences in your Weekly Concept Journal.

Who I helped: _____

_____

Why I helped: _____

_____

Why I liked helping: _____

_____

Vocabulary words I can use: _____

_____

ELA W 1.1 Create multiple-paragraph narrative compositions: a. Establish and develop a situation or plot. b. Describe the setting. c. Present an ending. (ELD W I2)

73

Vocabulary

PICTURE IT!

environment

PICTURE IT!

soared

conditions
conservation
contribute
endangered
investigation
protect

What can people do to protect wild animals?

Some wild animals are in trouble. People can help. They can talk to their leaders about new laws to protect animals. They can tell others about endangered animals. When people know about the problem, they can help solve it.

Vocabulary in Context

Read the passage together.
Then circle the vocabulary words.

Saving Bald Eagles

When settlers first came to America, thousands of bald eagles soared there. As more people arrived, bald eagles had fewer places left in their environment where they could make nests and hunt. The birds could not live in those conditions, and many died.

In the 1960s, scientists did an investigation of bald eagles. They discovered why the birds were dying out. Many groups began working toward the conservation of bald eagles. The government passed a law in 1973 to protect endangered animals. Bald eagles were listed as an endangered species in 1976.

Many people worked together to contribute to the effort to save bald eagles. In summer 2007, bald eagles were removed from the endangered species list.

. . . .

Talk About It How were bald eagles saved from dying out? Complete the sentences below.

> Scientists _____ and discovered _____.
>
> Many groups began working _____.
>
> In 1973, the government _____.

. . . .

Your Turn What might have happened to bald eagles if people had not worked to save them? Tell a partner what you think. Explain your opinion.

Expressing and Supporting Opinions We use words to express how we feel about something. When we say what we think about something, we express an opinion. It is important to support our opinions with facts or examples.

Example: **I believe** that it is important to protect bald eagles so that the species does not die out.

We use special words to signal that an opinion is being expressed.

Circle the words used to express opinions in the chart below.

I believe, I agree	I agree that we should protect endangered animals so that more species will be removed from the endangered species list.
I think, I don't think	I don't think anyone should be allowed to harm endangered species because hurting animals is wrong.
People shouldn't	People shouldn't pollute the environment because it harms many animals.
In my opinion	In my opinion, every country should have an Endangered Species Act so that all endangered animals will be protected.

Talk About It Say a sentence that expresses an opinion about protecting wild animals. Use the words above to help you. Tell your sentence to a partner.

Your Turn Write a sentence that expresses your opinion about protecting animals. Be sure to give a fact or example to support your opinion.

_____

_____

Fact and Opinion When we read, it is important to distinguish between **facts and opinions.** A fact tells something that can be proven true or false. An opinion tells the author's thoughts or feelings.

A fact can be proven true or false by reading, by personal experiences, or by asking an expert. A statement of opinion may have clue words such as *I think*, *I believe*, or *in my opinion*. The paragraph below has both facts and opinions.

Siberian tigers are endangered animals. They can be found in Russia, China, and North Korea. I think everyone should try to help protect them. They are very beautiful.

Talk About It Look at the paragraph above. Which sentences about the Siberian tiger are facts? Which sentences are opinions?

Complete the sentences below with a partner.

The sentence _____ is an opinion because _____ .

The sentence _____ is a fact because _____ .

Your Turn Think of an animal you know about. Write a fact and an opinion about that animal. Use words to signal an opinion is being expressed.

_____

_____

ELA R 2.5 Distinguish facts, supported inferences, and opinions in text. (ELD R EA15)

77

Grammar

Main and Helping Verbs A **main verb** is usually an action word. *Trying* and *protect* are main verbs. A **helping verb** works with the main verb. The helping verbs are circled in these examples.

Many people (were) trying to save the bald eagle.

We (can) protect endangered animals.

The chart below lists helping verbs.

Helping Verbs							
be	am	was	may	have	do	could	will
being	is	were	might	has	does	would	can
been	are		must	had	did	should	shall

Talk About It What are the main and helping verbs in these sentences?

José will study marine animals that are in danger.

Allie might see a Bengal tiger at the zoo.

Your Turn Circle the main verb and underline the helping verb in the sentence below.

A crocodile will swim away if you try to capture it.

ELA LC 1.2 Identify and correctly use verbs that are often misused (e.g., *lie/lay, sit/set, rise/raise*), modifiers, and pronouns. (ELD LC I8)

Think, Talk, and Write

Protecting Animals Think about how people worked together to save the bald eagle. Talk with a partner about ways people protect animals.

How does telling people about endangered animals help?

How does keeping the environment clean help?

Talk About It Review the vocabulary on page 74. Work with a partner to tell about each word. Which words will you use to write a letter to help protect an endangered animal?

Produce Language Write a letter to your congressperson to help protect an endangered animal. First complete the chart. Then write 5 to 6 sentences in your Weekly Concept Journal.

My animal: _____

_____

Why my animal is endangered: _____

_____

What people can do to help: _____

_____

Vocabulary words I can use: _____

_____

ELA W 2.4 Write persuasive letters or compositions: a. State a clear position in support of a proposal. b. Support a position with relevant evidence. c. Follow a simple organizational pattern. d. Address reader concerns. (ELD W I6)

79

Promoting Freedom

Vocabulary

educated

published

encouraged
enslaved
freedom
glimmer
promote

How can people promote freedom?

During the American Revolution, many people promoted freedom in different ways. Some people, like Phillis Wheatley, used writing to promote freedom.

Vocabulary in Context

Read the passage together.
Then circle the vocabulary words.

Phillis Wheatley

Phillis Wheatley brought the glimmer of hope to many enslaved people. She wrote poetry to promote freedom.

Not many enslaved people were educated. However, as a young girl, Wheatley learned to read and write. She was encouraged to write poetry. She published her first poem at the age of twelve.

In 1773, Wheatley became the first African American to publish a book of poems. That same year, Wheatley was freed from slavery. When she was free, Wheatley published a letter telling how slavery was wrong and a poem to George Washington. She believed that all people in America should be free.

Talk About It What are some of the most important things about Phillis Wheatley's life? Complete the sentences below.

> Wheatley brought hope to _____.
>
> She was the first _____.
>
> She believed that _____ and she wrote _____.

Your Turn How did Phillis Wheatley promote freedom? Tell a partner.

ELA R 1.4 Know abstract, derived roots and affixes from Greek and Latin and use this knowledge to analyze the meaning of complex words (e.g., *controversial*). (ELD R I8)

Sequencing Certain words and phrases show the order in which things happen. Sometimes things happen at the same time. We use special words, such as *during*, *while*, and *meanwhile*, to talk about events that happen at the same time.

Example: Phillis Wheatley was alive **during the American Revolution.**

Sometimes things happen over a period of time.
We use special words and phrases to indicate that
something happened over a period of time.

Example: **Between 1771 and 1773,**
Phillis Wheatley published many poems.

Circle the words that show when something happened.

when, in	In 1773, Phillis Wheatley published her first book.
while, during, meanwhile	While she was enslaved, Phillis Wheatley published her first poem at age 12.
between, still	People still talk about Phillis Wheatley because she was such an important woman in American history.

Talk About It Tell about a time when Phillis Wheatley promoted freedom. Use one word or phrase from the chart that tells when this happened.

Your Turn Write a sentence about another person who has promoted freedom in some way. Use one word or phrase that tells when this happened.

_____

Sequence It is important to understand the **sequence,** or order in which things happen, in a story or article. Dates, times of day, and certain words such as *first, next, last,* and *then* can give clues about the sequence.

Read the paragraph below. Circle the sequence words.

Between 1774 and early 1775, Paul Revere brought messages from Massachusetts to New York and Philadelphia. In April 1775, Revere was asked to warn Samuel Adams that the British troops were coming. Revere arrived in Lexington near midnight and gave Adams the message. He continued to Concord, where he was then arrested by the British.

Talk About It Look at the paragraph about Paul Revere. In what order did events happen?

Complete the sentences below with a partner.

Paul Revere was asked to warn Samuel Adams in _____.

He arrived in Lexington near _____ and then _____.

Your Turn Put the following sentences in the correct order. Circle what happened first. Underline what happened next. Draw a box around what happened last.

Paul Revere arrived in Lexington.

Paul Revere arrived in Concord.

Paul Revere was asked to warn Samuel Adams.

ELA R 2.2 Analyze text that is organized in sequential or chronological order. (ELD R EA16)

83

Grammar

Subject-Verb Agreement The **subjects** and **verbs** in a sentence should agree. When you have a singular subject, use a singular verb. When you have a plural subject, use a plural verb. Look at the chart below. There are examples of correct subject-verb agreement and incorrect subject-verb agreement.

Incorrect Subject-Verb Agreement	Correct Subject-Verb Agreement
Paul Revere are going to Lexington.	Paul Revere is going to Lexington.
Paul and other riders was brave.	Paul and other riders were brave.
Samuel Adams listen to the message.	Samuel Adams listens to the message.

Talk About It What is the subject in each sentence? Is the subject-verb agreement correct in the sentences below? Why or why not?

David run every day after school.

Our teacher are Mr. Jones.

Your Turn Underline the subject in each sentence below. Decide whether it is plural or singular, and then circle the correct verb.

Phillis Wheatley and Paul Revere are/is two people who promoted freedom.

Phillis Wheatley were/was an important woman.

We study/studies people who promoted freedom in school.

 ELA G6 LC 1.2 Identify and properly use indefinite pronouns and present perfect, past perfect, and future perfect verb tenses; ensure that verbs agree with compound subjects. (ELD LC EA8)

Think, Talk, and Write

Promoting Freedom Think about how Phillis Wheatley used her poems to promote freedom. Talk with a partner about other people who have promoted freedom.

How does Nelson Mandela promote freedom?

How did Princess Diana promote freedom?

. . . .

Talk About It Review the vocabulary on page 80. Work with a partner to tell about each word. Which words will you use to write about a person who promotes freedom?

. . . .

Produce Language Write about a person who promotes freedom. First complete the chart. Then write 5 to 6 sentences in your Weekly Concept Journal.

My person: _____

_____

How he or she promotes freedom: _____

_____

Who is helped: _____

_____

Vocabulary words I can use: _____

_____

ELA W 2.3 Write research reports about important ideas, issues, or events by using the following guidelines: a. Frame questions that direct the investigation. b. Establish a controlling idea or topic. c. Develop the topic with simple facts, details, examples, and explanations. (ELD W I3)

85

Get Online!
PearsonSuccessNet.com

Hear it!
See it!
Do it!

- Big Question Video
- Concept Talk Video
- Interactive Sound-
  Spelling Charts
- Picture It! Animation
- eBooks
- Grammar Jammer
- Online Journal

Inventors and Artists

What do people gain from the work of inventors and artists?

Unit 3

Inventors and Their Inventions
How do inventors inspire our imaginations?

Art and Artists
How do artists inspire future generations?

Dinosaurs and Paleontology
How can paleontologists help us understand the past?

Music and Musicians
How does an artist use music to inspire others?

Special Effects
How do artists create special effects to entertain us?

Vocabulary

PICTURE IT!

eyeglasses

PICTURE IT!

lightning rod

device
fabulous
gadgets
imagination
inspecting

How do inventors inspire our imaginations?

Ben Franklin was very curious about science and many other subjects. He had a fabulous imagination and invented many useful devices, most of which people still use today. Franklin was one of the greatest inventors of his time.

Vocabulary in Context

Read the passage together.
Then circle the vocabulary words.

Ben Franklin's Curious Mind

Ben Franklin was curious about many different subjects. He was constantly inspecting the world around him. His inventions changed the way people live.

Franklin invented all kinds of gadgets. He created the first swim fins, a special kind of eyeglasses, and even the first device that measures distance! One of his most important inventions, though, saved many lives.

Lightning started many fires in the 1700s. Franklin studied lightning and invented a way to protect people and buildings from lightning strikes. He created the lightning rod—a tall, iron rod placed on top of a building. Lightning would strike the rod and be sent into the ground instead of hitting the building and starting a fire. Franklin's lightning rod is still used today!

· ·

Talk About It How do Ben Franklin's inventions influence our lives today? Complete the sentences below.

Ben Franklin _____ many useful things.

Many of Franklin's inventions, such as _____, are still used today.

By inventing the _____ _____, Franklin saved _____ from getting struck by lightning.

· ·

Your Turn Think of an important invention.
Tell a partner why it is important.

Interpreting We use words to tell how we feel or what we think about something or someone. We may use special language to show that we feel strongly.

Example: Ben Franklin **always** did the right thing. He was the **best** inventor **that ever** lived. **No other** inventor was as good as he was.

We interpret words and sentences by telling what they mean. The strong language in these sentences shows that the author thinks that Ben Franklin was the best inventor.

Read the sentences below. Circle the words and phrases that show strong feelings.

most important	Inventors have the most important job in the world.
always	Inventors think they are always right.
should all	We should all be inventors.
best, that ever	It was the best invention that I have ever seen.

Talk About It Look at the three pictures of inventions. Choose the invention that you think is the most important. Say a sentence that shows you feel strongly about this invention. Use the words above to help you.

Your Turn Write a sentence about one of the inventions above. Use words that show you feel strongly about this invention.

_____

_____

Comprehension Support

Author's Viewpoint/Bias The **Author's viewpoint** is the way an author looks at the subject he or she is writing about. An author's viewpoint may be positive or negative. You can learn about an author's viewpoint by looking at the author's words and opinions.

Balanced writing includes positive and negative viewpoints on a subject. Unbalanced writing includes more information on one viewpoint than the other. Including more information on one viewpoint than the other is a form of **bias.** As you read, look for the author's viewpoint and possible bias.

Ben Franklin, Hero
Ben Franklin should be an inspiration for everyone. He spent his life learning new things. Ben Franklin started hospitals, fire departments, and colleges. He is the best role model. We should all try to be like Ben.

Talk About It How can you tell the author's viewpoint of Ben Franklin? Is the writing balanced? Why or why not?

Your Turn Look at the paragraph above. Write a sentence about Ben Franklin that could be interpreted as biased. Then, write a sentence that does *not* show bias.

_____

_____

Past, Present, and Future Tenses English has three basic verb tenses. The **past tense** tells what already happened. The **present tense** tells what is happening now. The **future tense** tells what will happen later. Examples of the three verb tenses are circled in the chart.

Past Tense	The inventor invented many helpful things.
Present Tense	An inventor invents things that help people.
Future Tense	An inventor will invent things that will help people.

Talk About It In which tense are the verbs in these sentences?

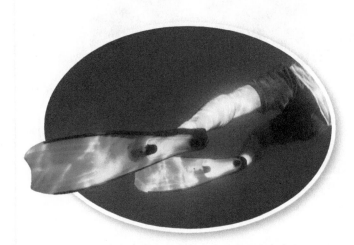

Ben Franklin invented swim fins.

The scientist observes germs through a microscope.

Your Turn Read each sentence. Fill in the blank with the correct tense of the verb *invent.*

Jim and Dora _____ video games at work.

Gary _____ a flying car next year.

Ella _____ a children's toy ten years ago.

ELA LC 1.2 Identify and correctly use verbs that are often misused (e.g., *lie/lay, sit/set, rise/raise*), modifiers, and pronouns. (ELD LC EA8)

Think, Talk, and Write

Inventors and Their Inventions Think about how Benjamin Franklin's inventions helped make life better. Talk with a partner about other inventions that have made life better.

How does the computer make life better?

How does the telephone make life better?

- -

Talk About It Review the vocabulary on page 88. Work with a partner to tell about each word. Which words will you use to write about an invention that has made your life better?

- -

Produce Language Use your imagination to think of an invention that will make your life better. First complete the chart. Then write 5 to 6 sentences in your Weekly Concept Journal.

My invention: _____

_____

My invention's purpose: _____

_____

How it makes my life better: _____

_____

Vocabulary words I can use: _____

_____

ELA W 1.2 Create multiple-paragraph expository compositions: a. Establish a topic, important ideas, or events in sequence or chronological order. b. Provide details and transitional expressions that link one paragraph to another in a clear line of thought. c. Offer a concluding paragraph that summarizes important ideas and details. (ELD W I5)

Art and Artists

Vocabulary

landscape

photographer

achieved
generations
midst
preserve
spectacular
talented

How do artists inspire future generations?

Ansel Adams was a famous photographer. He has inspired future generations of photographers with his spectacular black-and-white landscape photographs. He also inspired people to take care of the beautiful places in his photographs.

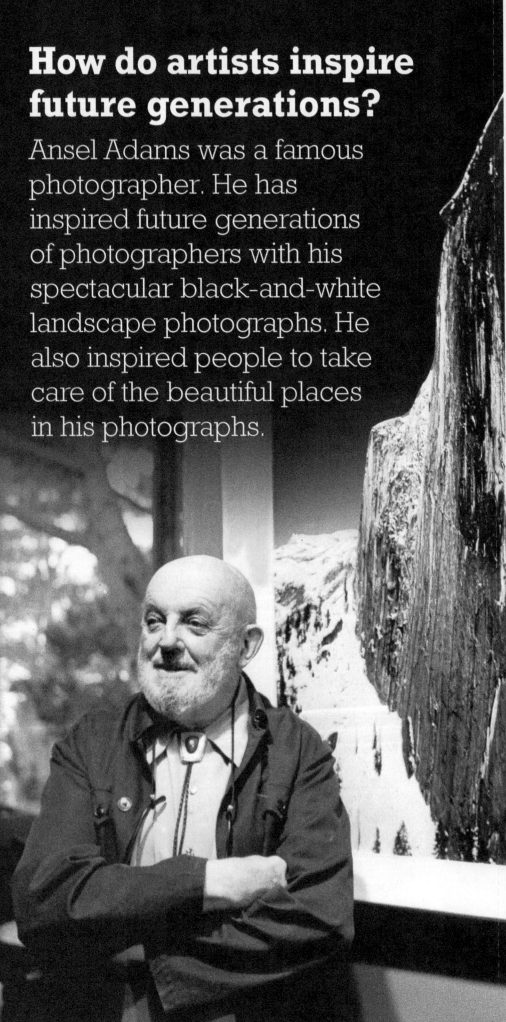

Read the passage together.
Then circle the vocabulary words.

Ansel Adams

From a young age, Ansel Adams loved being in nature. Then Adams received his first camera when he was fourteen. He later achieved great fame as a talented nature photographer.

Adams traveled all over the American West with his camera. In the midst of the wilderness, he took spectacular black-and-white photographs of mountains, canyons, and waterfalls. He wanted everyone to appreciate and preserve each beautiful landscape he photographed.

Adams used his photographs to show people the land he wanted to protect for future generations. He worked closely with environmental groups to save the American wilderness. He spoke with lawmakers, wrote articles, and helped to create a national park.

Talk About It How did Ansel Adams inspire others?
Complete the sentences below.

> Ansel Adams inspired others by _____.
>
> He used his photographs to _____.

Your Turn Think of an artist or someone you know who inspires you. How does he or she inspire you? Tell a partner.

ELA R 1.1 Read aloud narrative and expository text fluently and accurately and with appropriate pacing, intonation, and expression. (ELD R I2)

95

Language Workshop FORM & FUNCTION

Summarizing We use words to summarize, or tell the main points of what we have read or heard. When we summarize, we use special words, such as *in summary*, *indeed*, or *in other words*.

Example: Photography was not always thought of as fine art. People thought that paintings and sculptures were fine art. Ansel Adams showed people that photography can be fine art. **Indeed,** Ansel Adams inspired photographers to be artists.

Circle the special words used to summarize.

In summary	In summary, Ansel Adams changed the way people think about photography.
In other words	In other words, people thought that only painters and sculptors were artists.
Indeed	Indeed, Ansel Adams was an artist.

. . . .

Talk About It Say a sentence that summarizes the work of Ansel Adams. Use the words in the chart above to help you.

. . . .

Your Turn Write a sentence that summarizes what you think of Ansel Adams.

_____

_____

_____

_____

_____ *Evening Cloud*, Ellery Lake, Sierra Nevada, 1934 by Ansel Adams

ELA LC 1.1 Identify and correctly use prepositional phrases, appositives, and independent and dependent clauses; use transitions and conjunctions to connect ideas. (ELD LC EA8)

Main Idea The most important point in a text is the **main idea.**
The main idea is often stated at the beginning of the text, but can also
be stated in the middle or at the end of the text. The other sentences in a
paragraph are details that support the main idea. The paragraph below
contains a main idea and details.

Ansel Adams was very concerned
about taking care of our planet.
He took photographs of nature.
He used his photographs to help
people see the beauty of nature.
He wanted everyone to care
about preserving nature.

Talk About It What is the main idea in the paragraph above?
What is one detail that supports the main idea?

Complete the sentences below with a partner.

In summary, _____.

One detail that supports the main idea is _____.

Your Turn Underline the detail that supports the main idea that
Ansel Adams was an important artist.

He was born in California.

He inspired other photographers.

He got a camera when he was fourteen years old.

ELA R 2.3 Discern main ideas and concepts presented in texts, identifying and assessing evidence that supports those ideas. (ELD R I11)

97

Principal Parts of Regular Verbs English verbs have four forms. These forms tell what is happening now and what happened in the past. The forms are the **present,** the **past,** the **past participle,** and the **present participle.** The present participle and past participle are used with helping verbs.

Present	The girls paint a picture.
Past	The girls painted a picture.
Past Participle	The girls have painted a picture.
Present Participle	The girls are painting a picture.

Talk About It What is the form of the verb in each sentence?

The artist achieved great things.

The artist is achieving great things.

Your Turn Write three sentences. Use a different form of the verb *talk* in each sentence.

_____

_____

_____

ELA LC 1.2 Identify and correctly use verbs that are often misused (e.g., *lie/lay, sit/set, rise/raise*), modifiers, and pronouns. (ELD LC EA8)

Think, Talk, and Write

Art and Artists Think about how Ansel Adams' photographs have inspired others. Talk with a partner about how you might use photographs to inspire others.

Would you photograph lakes?

Would you photograph endangered animals?

Talk About It Review the vocabulary on page 94. Work with a partner to tell about each word. Which words will you use to write about art that inspires you?

Produce Language Write about some art that has inspired you. First complete the chart. Then write 5 to 6 sentences in your Weekly Concept Journal.

My art: _____

_____

The subject: _____

_____

How it inspires me: _____

_____

Vocabulary words I can use: _____

_____

ELA W 2.3 Write research reports about important ideas, issues, or events by using the following guidelines: a. Frame questions that direct the investigation. b. Establish a controlling idea or topic. c. Develop the topic with simple facts, details, examples, and explanations. (ELD W I3)

99

Vocabulary

PICTURE IT!
dinosaur

PICTURE IT!
fossil

PICTURE IT!
skeleton

embryo

occasion

paleontologists

roam

How can paleontologists help us understand the past?

Paleontologists discover and study plant and animal fossils. Fossils help us learn about the history of Earth.

Read the passage together.
Then circle the vocabulary words.

JACK HORNER, PALEONTOLOGIST

Jack Horner was born on June 15, 1946, in Montana. Jack found his first dinosaur fossil when he was only six years old. Since that time, he has found many, many more dinosaur fossils.

On one occasion when Jack was searching for fossils, he discovered the first dinosaur embryo. Imagine a dinosaur egg with a baby dinosaur skeleton inside!

Jack Horner also discovered Maiasaura—a dinosaur that lived 77 million years ago. Nests and eggs were found in the area where Maiasaura used to roam. This told paleontologists that these dinosaurs cared for their young. Because of this, Horner gave Maiasaura a name that means "good mother lizard."

. . . .

Talk About It Why were Jack Horner's discoveries important? Complete the sentences below.

> Jack Horner discovered a _____
> with a _____ inside.
>
> Paleontologists learned _____ from Maiasaura.

. . . .

Your Turn How are paleontologists able to teach us about the past? Tell a partner what you think.

Expressing and Supporting Opinions We use words to tell our opinion. If we support an opinion, we say *I agree...*

Example: **I agree** that Jack Horner is an important paleontologist.

If we do not support an opinion, we say *I disagree...*

Example: People should stop wasting time studying old fossils. **I disagree.** Learning about the past helps us to understand the present.

- -

Talk About It Say a sentence that tells that you agree or disagree with this sentence: *It would be exciting to be a paleontologist.*

Complete one of the sentences below.

I agree that _____.

I disagree that _____.

- -

Your Turn   Write a sentence that tells if you agree or disagree with the following statement: *Paleontologists do very important work.*

_____

_____

Fact and Opinion A statement of **fact** tells something that can be proven true or false. A statement that tells how a person feels about something is a statement of **opinion.** A statement of opinion can be true or false, but cannot be proven.

Example: **Opinion:** I believe it is fun to explore caves.
Fact: That is a very old cave.

. . . .

Talk About It Read the sentences in the example above. Why is the first statement an opinion? Why is the second statement a fact? Do you agree or disagree with the opinion?

Complete one of the sentences below.

I agree because _____ .

I disagree because _____ .

. . . .

Your Turn Read the sentences. Underline the fact. Circle the opinion.

Maiasaura was a plant-eating dinosaur.

Maiasaura is the most interesting dinosaur.

ELA R 2.5 Distinguish facts, supported inferences, and opinions in text. (ELD R EA15)

103

Grammar

Principal Parts of Irregular Verbs The principal parts of regular verbs are formed by adding *-d, -ed,* or *-ing*. The **principal parts of irregular verbs** are formed in a different way. The spelling of the irregular verb is changed.

Verb Tense	Irregular Verbs	Regular Verbs
Present	Paleontologists (dig) holes.	Paleontologists (discover) dinosaurs.
Past	Paleontologists (dug) holes.	Paleontologists (discovered) dinosaurs.
Past Participle	Paleontologists (have dug) holes.	Paleontologists (have discovered) dinosaurs.
Present Participle	Paleontologists (are digging) holes.	Paleontologists (are discovering) dinosaurs.

. . . .

Talk About It What are the irregular verbs in these sentences? Circle the irregular verb in each sentence.

James spoke to a paleontologist who studies fossils.

Rita has seen a T-rex skeleton in a museum.

. . . .

Your Turn Finish these sentences. Use a form of the irregular verb *dig*.

Right now, Julie _____ for fossils.

Julie _____ for fossils yesterday.

🐻 **ELA LC 1.2** Identify and correctly use verbs that are often misused (e.g., *lie/lay, sit/set, rise/raise*), modifiers, and pronouns. (ELD LC EA8)

Think, Talk, and Write

Dinosaurs and Paleontology Think about how Jack Horner's discoveries helped us learn about dinosaurs. Talk with a friend about what we learn from paleontologists.

What can you learn from this fossil?

What can you learn from this dinosaur?

- -

Talk About It Review the vocabulary on page 100. Work with a partner to tell about each word. Which words will you use to write about why paleontologists' work is important?

- -

Produce Language Write about why paleontologists' work is important. First complete the chart below. Then write 5 to 6 sentences in your Weekly Concept Journal.

Things paleontologists can discover: _____

_____

Why paleontologists' work is important: _____

_____

Things I'd like paleontologists to learn about: _____

_____

Vocabulary words I can use: _____

_____

ELA W 2.4 Write persuasive letters or compositions: a. State a clear position in support of a proposal. b. Support a position with relevant evidence. c. Follow a simple organizational pattern. d. Address reader concerns. (ELD W EA2)

105

Vocabulary

cornet

trumpet

appreciate

impressed

jazz

serious

soloist

style

How does an artist use music to inspire others?

Louis Armstrong grew up in New Orleans, Louisiana. He learned to appreciate music when he was very young. He was inspired by the jazz music that he heard all over the city.

Vocabulary in Context

Read the passage together.
Then circle the vocabulary words.

Louis Armstrong

Louis Armstrong is known as one of the best jazz musicians of all time. People today still appreciate his joyful music and sense of humor. He was the first great jazz trumpet soloist. Later he also earned fame as a singer.

Armstrong loved music from a young age. He bought an old, used cornet when he was a teenager and became serious about music. Older musicians were impressed with his talent and helped him. He later became one of the best trumpet players in the world.

Armstrong also invented a new style of singing. One day when he was singing, he made up sounds because he did not know the words to the song. This style of singing later became known as scat.

. . . .

Talk About It Why was Louis Armstrong an important musician? Complete the sentences below with a partner.

> Louis Armstrong was a talented _____ and _____ player.
>
> Louis Armstrong is famous for _____ .

. . . .

Your Turn Think of your favorite kind of music. Why is this music important to you? Tell a partner.

ELA R 1.1 Read aloud narrative and expository text fluently and accurately and with appropriate pacing, intonation, and expression. (ELD R I2)

107

Language Workshop FORM & FUNCTION

Summarizing When we summarize, we tell the main point of what we see, hear, or read. When we summarize, we use words that tell who, what, when, how, and sometimes why. The sentence below tells who, what, and how.

Example: Louis Armstrong played the trumpet very well.

. . . .

Talk About It Look at the picture of jazz musicians.
Use words that tell who and what.

Complete the sentence below with a partner.

> The _____ are _____ .

. . . .

Your Turn Write a sentence that tells the main point of the picture.
Use words that tell who, what, how, and why.

_____

_____

ELA LC 1.1 Identify and correctly use prepositional phrases, appositives, and independent and dependent clauses; use transitions and conjunctions to connect ideas. (ELD LC EA8)

Comprehension Support

Main Idea The **main idea** is the most important idea about a topic. Sometimes the main idea is stated in the first sentence of a passage. Other times the main idea is stated in the middle or at the end of a passage. Sentences that tell about the main idea are supporting details.

Read the paragraph below. Look for details that support the main idea.

Louis Armstrong was a great jazz musician. He was a fantastic trumpet player. Louis invented scat. Scat is singing words that do not make sense. Though he died in 1971, his music continues to play around the world.

. . . .

Talk About It Tell the main idea in the paragraph above. What is one detail that supports the main idea? Use words that tell who, what, when, and how.

Complete the sentences with a partner.

> Louis Armstrong was a _____.
>
> One detail that supports the main idea is _____.

. . . .

Your Turn Underline the detail that supports the main idea that Louis Armstrong was an important jazz musician.

He was born in Louisiana.

He invented a style of singing called scat.

He had a sense of humor.

ELA R 2.3 Discern main ideas and concepts presented in texts, identifying and assessing evidence that supports those ideas. (ELD R I11)

109

Grammar

Troublesome Verbs Some verbs are **troublesome verbs.** They may sound like other verbs. The verbs *sit* and *set* can be troublesome. A person or animal *sits* down to rest. *Set* means to "put an object down."

Sit	Set
He needs to (sit) down and rest.	Please (set) the trumpet on the table.

Talk About It Use the correct form of *sit* or *set* in the sentences.

The musicians _____ down while they play.

Please _____ the drum on the floor.

Your Turn Write one sentence using the verb *set*. Write one sentence using the verb *sit*.

_____

_____

_____

_____

ELA LC 1.2 Identify and correctly use verbs that are often misused (e.g., *lie/lay, sit/set, rise/raise*), modifiers, and pronouns. (ELD LC EA8)

Think, Talk, and Write

Music and Musicians Think about how Louis Armstrong loved the cornet as a child and became a professional musician. Talk with a partner about the music that inspires you.

Does guitar music inspire you?

Does piano music inspire you?

Talk About It Review the vocabulary on page 106. Work with a partner to tell about each word. Which words will you use to write about how music inspires you?

Produce Language Write about the kind of music that inspires you. First complete the chart. Then write 5 to 6 sentences in your Weekly Concept Journal.

My favorite music: _____

_____

Why it inspires me: _____

_____

Why others should listen: _____

_____

Vocabulary words I can use: _____

_____

ELA W 2.4 Write persuasive letters or compositions: a. State a clear position in support of a proposal. b. Support a position with relevant evidence. c. Follow a simple organizational pattern. d. Address reader concerns. (ELD W EA5)

111

Vocabulary

gorilla

skyscraper

entertain
joints
menacing
miniature
model

How do artists create special effects to entertain us?

Artists use special effects to entertain us. They can use special effects to create illusions that seem real, such as the giant gorilla in *King Kong*.

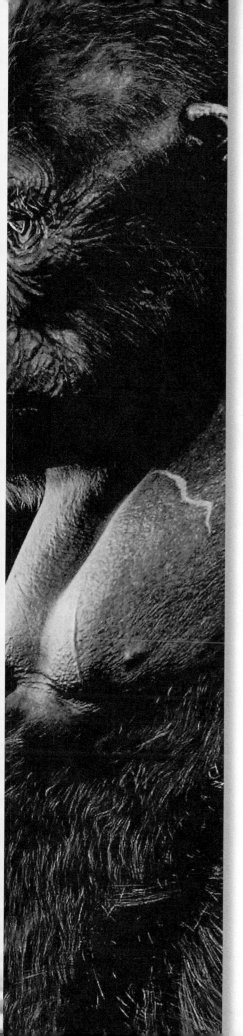

Read the passage together.
Then circle the vocabulary words.

King Kong

On the big screen, King Kong is a huge, menacing gorilla. His footsteps shake the ground like earthquakes. He is able to pick up cars and throw them like toys. He can climb a towering skyscraper. However, the gorilla in *King Kong* was really only eighteen inches tall!

One way artists create special effects is to make a miniature model. King Kong was a model that was covered with fur and had joints that could move. For the movie, artists also created a miniature model of the landscape of San Francisco. The buildings they created were only twelve feet tall. On the movie screen, the gorilla and buildings look real!

Talk About It How do artists make movies exciting? Complete the sentences below.

By using special effects, such as _____, artists can make _____ objects look large.

Models were used in *King Kong* to make _____.

Your Turn Think of a movie you know. What special effects did it have? Tell a partner about the movie.

ELA R 1.1 Read aloud narrative and expository text fluently and accurately and with appropriate pacing, intonation, and expression. (ELD R I1)

113

Language Workshop

Defining We tell what words mean when we define them.
Some words help to tell about other words.

Example: A skyscraper is a building.
A gorilla is an animal.

Words that describe, such as *tiny*, *small*,
big, *huge*, *gigantic*, *short*, and *tall* tell
the size of things.

Example: The **huge** gorilla climbed
the **tall** skyscraper.

. . . .

Talk About It Look at the picture of the skyscraper. Say a sentence that
defines a skyscraper. Use words that describe to tell more about a skyscraper.

Complete the sentences with a partner.

> A skyscraper is a _____ building with _____ .
>
> A skyscraper has _____ and _____ .

. . . .

Your Turn Write a sentence that tells what a gorilla is.
Use words that describe and define.

_____

_____

_____

ELA LC 1.2 Identify and correctly use verbs that are often misused (e.g., *lie/lay, sit/set, rise/raise*), modifiers, and pronouns. (ELD LC I8)

Graphic Sources Maps, diagrams, photographs, timelines, and storyboards are examples of **graphic sources.** Often graphics have words or labels to explain the information in them. Graphics may help you define something further. We can use words that describe to tell what a graphic is showing.

Storyboard

Talk About It What is happening in the story? How does the storyboard help you to understand what is happening?

> In scene 1, people are _____.
>
> In scene 2, a _____ gorilla is _____.
>
> In scene 3, the _____ gorilla is _____.

Your Turn Think of a scene from your favorite movie. Draw a storyboard to show what happens. Tell a partner about the scene.

ELA R 2.1 Understand how text features (e.g., format, graphics, sequence, diagrams, illustrations, charts, maps) make information accessible and usable. (ELD R I10)

115

Prepositions **Prepositions** are words that often tell where. Examples of prepositions include the words *above, across, in, behind, near,* and *under.*

The gorilla is (on) the skyscraper.   The gorilla is (near) the skyscraper.

Talk About It What are the prepositions in these sentences?
Circle the prepositions.

> The gorilla ran across the street.
>
> The miniature gorilla model is beside the building models.

Your Turn Write two sentences using prepositions that tell where.

The gorilla _____

_____

The skyscraper _____

_____

ELA LC 1.1 Identify and correctly use prepositional phrases, appositives, and independent and dependent clauses; use transitions and conjunctions to connect ideas. (ELD LC I8)

Think, Talk, and Write

Special Effects Think about how different the King Kong movie would be without special effects. Talk with a partner about other special effects you have seen in movies.

How does make-up create special effects?

How does animation create special effects?

Talk About It Review the vocabulary on page 112. Work with a partner to tell about each word. Which words will you use to write about your favorite movie that used special effects?

Produce Language Write about your favorite movie that used special effects. First complete the chart. Then write 5 to 6 sentences in your Weekly Concept Journal.

My movie: _____

_____

The special effects: _____

_____

Why I like it: _____

_____

Vocabulary words I can use: _____

_____

ELA W 2.3 Write research reports about important ideas, issues, or events by using the following guidelines: a. Frame questions that direct the investigation. b. Establish a controlling idea or topic. c. Develop the topic with simple facts, details, examples, and explanations. (ELD W I4)

Hear it!
See it!
Do it!

- Big Question Video
- Concept Talk Video
- Interactive Sound-
  Spelling Charts
- Picture It! Animation
- eBooks
- Grammar Jammer
- Online Journal

Adapting

How do people and
animals adapt to
different situations?

Unit 4

People Adapting
How do people adapt to difficult situations?

Adapting to Face Challenges
How do people adapt to face challenges?

Animal Adaptations
How do animals adapt to survive?

Adapting to a New Place
How do people adapt to a new school?

Improving Ourselves
Why do people try to change themselves?

Adapting

Vocabulary

oxen

pioneer

wagon

adapt
civilization
inspired
situations
supplies

How do people adapt to difficult situations?

Sometimes people face difficult situations. They might face bad weather or travel far from home. When people moved west in the 1800s, they adapted by doing things in new ways.

Vocabulary in Context

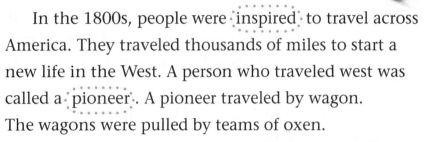

Read the passage together.
Then circle the vocabulary words.

Moving West

In the 1800s, people were inspired to travel across America. They traveled thousands of miles to start a new life in the West. A person who traveled west was called a pioneer. A pioneer traveled by wagon. The wagons were pulled by teams of oxen.

These pioneers had to adapt to many new situations. When there was little food or supplies, pioneers had to find new things to eat. When there was little water, pioneers had to find safe water to drink. When the weather was bad, pioneers had to protect themselves and their wagons. Life along a wagon trail was different from the civilization the pioneers had left behind.

Talk About It How did the pioneers adapt to difficult situations? Complete the sentences below.

> Some difficult situations were _____
> and _____ .
>
> When _____ , pioneers _____ .
>
> When _____ , pioneers _____ .

Your Turn Tell a partner how you adapted to a new situation. Use the sentence below to help.

When _____ , I adapted
by _____ .

ELA R 1.1 Read aloud narrative and expository text fluently and accurately and with appropriate pacing, intonation, and expression. (ELD R I1)

121

Draw Conclusions A conclusion is a decision you make when you think about facts and details. We draw conclusions when we compare two things. We can use *-er* words to compare.

Example: Tyler looked at the large tree. It was **taller** than the last tree he cut down. Tyler thought cutting down this tree would be **harder** than cutting down the last tree.

Circle the words that are used to compare in the sentences below.

Sara looked at the ox and the calf. The calf was smaller than the ox. Sara thought the ox would be much stronger because it was bigger than the calf.

- -

Talk About It Use *-er* words to compare the men in these pictures.

- -

Your Turn Write a sentence that compares the two men above. Use *-er* words.

_____

_____

_____

ELA LC 1.2 Identify and correctly use verbs that are often misused (e.g., *lie/lay, sit/set, rise/raise*), modifiers, and pronouns. (ELD LC I8)

Draw Conclusions To **draw conclusions,** you use what you already know and details you read or see to make decisions. When you draw conclusions, you sometimes use *-er* words to compare people or things.

What conclusions can you draw from this picture?

Talk About It Talk with a partner about the picture above. Draw conclusions about what the pioneers are doing. Complete the sentences below with a partner.

> The woman is growing food because _____.
>
> The man is chopping wood because _____.
>
> _____ is _____er than _____.

Your Turn Reread the passage on page 121. What conclusions can you draw about pioneer life? Use *-er* words to compare life on the wagon trail to life in civilization.

_____

_____

_____

ELA R 2.4 Draw inferences, conclusions, or generalizations about text and support them with textual evidence and prior knowledge. (ELD R EI12)

123

Subject Pronouns In English, we sometimes use pronouns to take the place of nouns. A **subject pronoun** takes the place of the subject in a sentence.

	Singular	**Plural**
First person	(I) gather wood for a fire.	(We) build a fire.
Second person	(You) walk next to the covered wagon.	(You) ride in the covered wagon.
Third person	(He) plants tomatoes. (She) plants corn. (It) is a nice garden.	(They) help plant the garden.

Talk About It Read the sentences. Circle the subject pronouns.

She stirs the soup in the pot.

They gather wood for a fire.

Your Turn The subject of each sentence is circled. Change the subject to a subject pronoun. Then use a subject pronoun to write a sentence of your own.

(Grandmother and I) bake a pie. _____

(John) builds a log cabin. _____

(The wagon) has a broken wheel. _____

_____

_____

Think, Talk, and Write

People Adapting Think about how the pioneers adapted to life on the wagon trail. Talk with a partner about other times when people have to adapt.

How do people adapt to bad weather?

How do people adapt to traveling?

- -

Talk About It Review the vocabulary on page 120. Work with a partner to tell about each word. Which words will you use to write about how someone would adapt to living somewhere else?

- -

Produce Language Write about how you would adapt to living away from civilization. First complete the chart. Then write 5 to 6 sentences in your Weekly Concept Journal.

Where I would live: _____ _____
How I would adapt: _____ _____
How it would feel: _____ _____
Vocabulary words I can use: _____ _____

ELA W 1.1 Create multiple-paragraph narrative compositions: a. Establish and develop a situation or plot. b. Describe the setting. c. Present an ending. (ELD W I2)

125

Vocabulary

PICTURE IT!

newspaper

PICTURE IT!

printing press

accurate

challenge

critical

extraordinary

print

How do people adapt to face challenges?

People adapt to challenges. A challenge could be learning something new, such as a language. A challenge could also be a change, such as moving to a new place. John Peter Zenger adapted to face challenges when he came to America.

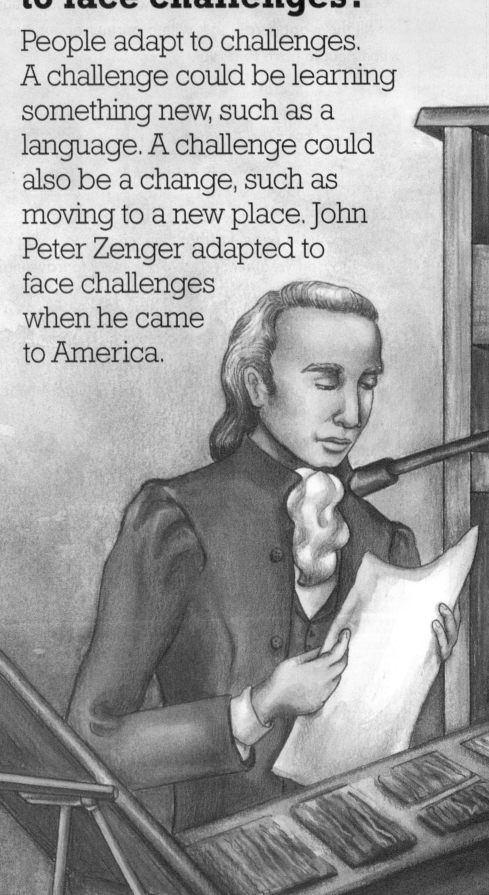

Vocabulary in Context

Read the passage together.
Then circle the vocabulary words.

John Peter Zenger: Newspaper Man

John Peter Zenger was born in 1710 in Germany. As a boy, he moved to America. Moving was a (challenge), but he learned to adapt to living in a new place. He learned how to (print) and use a printing press. Then, in 1733, he did an extraordinary thing. He began New York's first newspaper.

Zenger wanted to print news that was true and accurate. His newspaper printed many critical things about the governor. The governor did not like this and sent Zenger to jail. However, Zenger showed that his newspaper had printed the truth. Since then, U.S. news-papers have been granted freedom of the press. Zenger is remembered as one of the greatest men in early America.

. . . .

Talk About It What challenges did Zenger face? Complete the sentences below.

> Two challenges that John Peter Zenger faced were _____ and _____ .
>
> Because Zenger _____ , he _____ .

. . . .

Your Turn Write about a challenge that you have faced.

Use the sentence frames to help.

A challenge I faced was _____ .

I adapted by _____ .

Language Workshop FORM & FUNCTION

Persuading When we try to persuade people, we try to get them to believe or do something. We persuade by giving reasons. We often use the word *if* when we try to persuade people.

Example: **If you vote for Henry,** he will make our school newspaper better.
If you work hard, you will be able to adapt to a challenge.

In the example above, we give a reason to persuade people to vote for Henry.

Circle the phrases used to persuade in the sentences below.

The newspaper will be great if you work very hard.

If you write a good story, Henry will print it.

If you stay late, I will help you.

Talk About It Say a sentence that persuades someone to do something. What words did you use to persuade?

Complete the sentences below.

If you _____, you will _____.

If you _____, I will _____.

Your Turn Write a sentence that persuades a friend to do something. Underline the words that you used to persuade.

_____

_____

ELA LS 1.2 Interpret a speaker's verbal and nonverbal messages, purposes, and perspectives. (ELD LS I1)

Author's Viewpoint/Bias An **author's viewpoint** is the way an author thinks about a topic. A **bias** is a very strong feeling for or against something. For example, when John Peter Zenger's newspaper criticized the governor, some people said the newspaper was biased against the governor.

If You Vote for Governor Crosby, You Will Pay Higher Taxes

Go

- -

Talk About It What is the viewpoint of the author of the article above? Do you think it shows bias? Why?

Complete the sentences below.

> The author's viewpoint is _____.
>
> I think it does show bias because _____.
>
> I think it does not show bias because _____.

- -

Your Turn Reread the last sentence of the passage on page 127, "Zenger is remembered as one of the greatest men in early America."

Does this sentence show bias? Write why or why not.

_____

_____

_____

ELA R 3.7 Evaluate the author's use of various techniques (e.g., appeal of characters in a picture book, logic and credibility of plots and settings, use of figurative language) to influence readers' perspectives. (ELD R I16)

129

Grammar

Pronouns and Antecedents **Pronouns** are words that take the place of nouns. Some pronouns are *I, you, he, she,* and *it*. A list of pronouns is on page 124. An **antecedent** is the noun that the pronoun takes the place of.

Look at the sentence below. *John* is the antecedent and *he* is the pronoun.

John faced a new challenge. He was going to make a birdhouse.

antecedent   pronoun

· ·

Talk About It Look at the circled pronouns in each sentence. What is the antecedent for each pronoun?

Louisa checked the math problems. She wanted to make sure the answers were accurate.

The first printing press was made in the 1400s. It was very different from printing presses today.

· ·

Your Turn Complete the sentences. Write the pronoun that goes with each underlined antecedent.

<u>John Peter Zenger</u> did not think _____ would go to jail for printing a newspaper.

<u>Rachel and Linda</u> knew that _____ would have to adapt to hot weather when they moved to Florida.

ELA LC 1.2 Identify and correctly use verbs that are often misused (e.g., *lie/lay, sit/set, rise/raise*), modifiers, and pronouns. (ELD LC EA8)

Think, Talk, and Write

Adapting to Face Challenges Think about how John Peter Zenger adapted to the challenge of owning a newspaper in America. Talk with a partner about other people who have faced big challenges.

How did Shirley Chisholm face challenges?

How did Elie Wiesel face challenges?

- -

Talk About It Review the vocabulary on page 126. Work with a partner to tell about each word. Which words will you use to write about a person who has faced big challenges?

- -

Produce Language Write about a person who has faced challenges. First complete the chart. Then write 5 to 6 sentences in your Weekly Concept Journal.

My person: _____

_____

Challenges my person faced: _____

_____

How my person adapted: _____

_____

Vocabulary words I can use: _____

_____

ELA W 1.2 Create multiple-paragraph expository compositions: a. Establish a topic, important ideas, or events in sequence or chronological order. b. Provide details and transitional expressions that link one paragraph to another in a clear line of thought. c. Offer a concluding paragraph that summarizes important ideas and details. (ELD W I5)

PICTURE IT!

habitat

adaptation
defense
enables
scarce
specialize

How do animals adapt to survive?

Special body parts help animals to survive. Animals change to be able to stay alive in different conditions. This change is called an adaptation. An adaptation helps animals when they are in danger or when food is scarce.

Vocabulary in Context

Read the passage together.
Then circle the vocabulary words.

The Red-Eyed Tree Frog

The red-eyed tree frog lives in a rainforest habitat. This frog has adapted to survive. It has body parts that specialize in defense and in finding food.

Defense

The red-eyed tree frog's eyes help it to survive. The frog sleeps during the day. When another animal comes near, the frog opens its eyes. Their red color scares the other animal away! This body part helps save the tree frog from being eaten by other animals.

Finding Food

The bottoms of the tree frog's feet are sticky. The feet stick to tree trunks, branches, and leaves of trees. This enables the frog to find food more easily in the trees.

. . . .

Talk About It What body parts help the tree frog to survive?

Complete the sentences below.

> The tree frog uses its special _____ to survive.
>
> The tree frog's feet _____ and _____.
>
> The tree frog's eyes _____ and _____.

. . . .

Your Turn Think of your favorite animal. How do its body parts help it to survive? Tell a partner about your animal. Use the example above to help you.

Describing We use words to describe things. When we describe the body parts of an animal, we tell what the parts are. We may describe what the parts do. We may also tell where the parts are.

Example: The tree frog's orange, sticky feet are **on top of the branch.**

on top of the branch

We can use words that answer the question *where?* to tell where the parts are.

Circle the words that answer the question *where?* in the sentences below.

on top of, above	The tree frog's orange, sticky feet are on top of the branch.
on the front of	The tree frog's red eyes are on the front of its head.
beside, next to	The tree frog's back feet are beside its front feet on the branch.
beneath, under, below	The tree frog's body is white beneath its mouth.

Talk About It Say a sentence that describes the parts of the tree frog. Use the words above to tell where each part is.

Your Turn Write a sentence that describes the parts of the tree frog in this picture. Include words that tell where each part is.

_____

_____

_____

ELA LC 1.1 Identify and correctly use prepositional phrases, appositives, and independent and dependent clauses; use transitions and conjunctions to connect ideas. (ELD LC I8)

Comprehension Support

Graphic Sources We use **graphic sources** to show information. A photograph is a graphic source. A diagram is a graphic source. Photographs and diagrams help show parts of animals or other things. We can use words that answer the question *where?* to talk about diagrams.

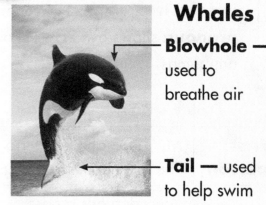

Whales

Blowhole — used to breathe air

Tail — used to help swim

Often graphic sources have labels. Labels give information about the graphic source. Labels can show where things are.

Circle the labels in the graphic source for whales.

· ·

Talk About It Look at the graphic source about whales. What information does the graphic source give you about whales?

Complete the sentences below with a partner.

> Whales have _____ and _____.
>
> A whale uses _____ on top of its head to _____.
>
> Without its _____, a whale could not survive.

· ·

Your Turn Look at the photograph and diagram of the fish. Write two sentences to tell about the graphic sources. Use words that answer the question *where?*

_____

_____

_____

_____

diagram

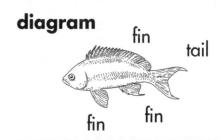

fin   tail

fin   fin

ELA R 2.1 Understand how text features (e.g., format, graphics, sequence, diagrams, illustrations, charts, maps) make information accessible and usable. (ELD R EA13)

135

Grammar

Possessive Pronouns Pronouns take the place of nouns. A **possessive pronoun** shows ownership. Possessive pronouns are used to describe people and things.

	Singular	**Plural**
First person	My book about tree frogs is long. The book about tree frogs is mine.	Our special hands help us hold pens. Those pens are ours.
Second person	Your dog has a nose that can smell food easily. Is that dog yours?	Your dogs all have special noses. Are those dogs yours?
Third person	His frog has sticky feet. Her frog has sticky feet. Its adaptations help it survive. This frog is his. This frog is hers.	Their fish have special fins. Those fish are not theirs.

. . . .

Talk About It Read the sentences and circle the possessive pronouns.

This bear has an adaptation.
Its fur keeps it warm.

These foxes also have special fur. Theirs helps them hide.

. . . .

Your Turn Finish the sentences. Use possessive pronouns from the chart.

Green bugs hide on the leaves of the tree in _____ yard.

Can you find any animals with adaptations in _____ book?

ELA LC 1.2 Identify and correctly use verbs that are often misused (e.g., *lie/lay, sit/set, rise/raise*), modifiers, and pronouns. (ELD LC EA8)

Think, Talk, and Write

Animal Adaptations Think about how the red-eyed tree frog adapts to survive. Talk with a partner about other animals that adapt to survive.

How does a camel adapt to survive?

How does a zebra adapt to survive?

Talk About It Review the vocabulary on page 132. Work with a partner to tell about each word. Which words will you use to write about animals adapting to survive?

Produce Language Write about an animal and how it adapts to survive. First complete the chart. Then write 5 to 6 sentences in your Weekly Concept Journal.

My animal: _____

_____

My animal's habitat: _____

_____

My animal's special body part: _____

_____

Vocabulary words I can use: _____

_____

ELA W 2.3 Write research reports about important ideas, issues, or events by using the following guidelines: a. Frame questions that direct the investigation. b. Establish a controlling idea or topic. c. Develop the topic with simple facts, details, examples, and explanations. (ELD W I3)

Adapting to a New Place

Vocabulary

American Revolution

assessment

assignment
combination
memorize
nervous
strict

How do people adapt to a new school?

Your first day at school might have been exciting or it might have been scary. Some students come from faraway places. New students have to learn to adapt to a new place and new people. Some even have to adapt to strict teachers.

Vocabulary in Context

Read the passage together.
Then circle the vocabulary words.

Maria's First Day

Scene I: Inside a social studies classroom

Mrs. Caldwell: Remember that a combination of events caused the American Revolution. For homework, please complete page 54. If you do not complete the assignment, you will have twice as much homework tomorrow night.

Maria (*sighing and gathering up her books*): Paulo, is Mrs. Caldwell always this strict?

Paulo: Yes, but she's a great teacher. She makes it fun to learn. She wants us to do more than memorize dates and facts.

Maria: Being new to this school makes me nervous. I will need to study more. I also think next week's assessment will be difficult. Will you help me?

Paulo: Sure. We can study together.

Maria: Paulo, that would be great! Thanks!

- -

Talk About It How will Maria adapt to her new school? Complete the sentence below.

Maria will adapt to the new school by _____ .

- -

Your Turn Think about your first day at school. Tell a partner how you adapted to your new school.

Generalizing When we generalize, we tell something we think is true, based on many examples. Many generalizations are about abstract nouns. Abstract nouns are things we cannot touch, such as beauty and love.

Read the generalizations below. Circle the abstract nouns.

> The beauty of nature is endless.
> Money does not bring happiness.
> People appreciate honesty.

Talk About It What are some other generalizations that use abstract nouns?

Work with a partner to use the following abstract nouns in generalizations: *joy*, *fear*, and *excitement*.

> Joy is _____.
>
> Fear is _____.
>
> Excitement is _____.

Your Turn Write a generalization about happiness.

Happiness is _____

_____

_____.

ELA LC 1.1 Identify and correctly use prepositional phrases, appositives, and independent and dependent clauses; use transitions and conjunctions to connect ideas. (ELD LC EA8)

Generalize Sometimes you can use information to **generalize** about what you read. Generalizations help you understand what you read.

Example: Sylvia thinks our teacher is strict. Alice thinks our teacher is strict. David thinks our teacher is strict.

After reading these sentences, I can generalize: Many students think the teacher is strict.

The word *many* is a clue that shows the sentence is a generalization. Other clue words are *some, most, always, sometimes,* and *never.*

. . . .

Talk About It Read the sentences below. What generalizations can you make about how Margo and her brother each felt? Talk with a partner.

> Margo walked quickly to school, wondering what her day would be like. She smiled, thinking about new friends she might meet. Her brother walked slowly behind. He frowned and stared at his shoes. He worried about what the assessments might be like.

. . . .

Your Turn Reread the passage on page 139. How can you generalize about adapting to a new school?

Write a generalization about adapting to a new school.

    Adapting to a new school is _____

    because _____ .

ELA R 2.4 Draw inferences, conclusions, or generalizations about text and support them with textual evidence and prior knowledge.
(ELD R I16)

141

Grammar

Indefinite Pronouns A pronoun is a word used in place of a noun. An **indefinite pronoun** does not refer to a specific noun. Indefinite pronouns include *something, someone, anything,* and *anyone.*

Does **anyone** have the pencils?
Someone has the pencils.

You can have **anything** you want for dinner.
Can we have **something** healthy to eat?

- -

Talk About It What are the indefinite pronouns in these sentences?

Work with a partner to read the sentences and circle the indefinite pronouns.

Does anyone know who our new teacher will be?

There will be someone new in our class this year.

Tell me something about yourself.

Is there anything we should do to get ready for the first day of school?

- -

Your Turn Complete the sentences. Use the indefinite pronouns listed above.

Anyone who turns in _____ for the project will get credit.

Does _____ know what the assignment is?

_____ has left her homework at home.

ELA LC 1.2 Identify and correctly use verbs that are often misused (e.g., *lie/ lay, sit/ set, rise/ raise*), modifiers, and pronouns. (ELD LC I8)

Think, Talk, and Write

Adapting to a New Place Think about how Maria adapted to her new school. Talk with a partner about other things Maria could do to adapt.

Could she join the band?

Could she make new friends?

Talk About It Review the vocabulary on page 138. Work with a partner to tell about each word. Which words will you use to write about how you adapted to a new place?

Produce Language Write about how you adapted to a new place. First complete the chart. Then write 5 to 6 sentences in your Weekly Concept Journal.

My new place: _____

_____

My feelings: _____

_____

How I adapted: _____

_____

Vocabulary words I can use: _____

_____

ELA W 2.1 Write narratives: a. Establish a plot, point of view, setting, and conflict. b. Show, rather than tell, the events of the story. (ELD W I3)

143

Vocabulary

PICTURE IT!
passengers

PICTURE IT!
steamship

hesitation
language
opportunities

Why do people try to change themselves?

People sometimes try to change. Some people change how they look. Some people change how they do things. Other people change where they live. They may move to find new opportunities, such as new jobs.

Vocabulary in Context

Read the passage together.
Then circle the vocabulary words.

Coming to the United States

In the early 1900s, many people from other countries moved to the United States. Immigrants came to the United States because they wanted opportunities, such as new jobs or a better place to live.

Many immigrants traveled across the Atlantic and Pacific Oceans as passengers on a steamship. These ships often carried hundreds of other immigrants. Even though the trip was going to be difficult, people traveled across the Atlantic Ocean to America without hesitation. They looked out over the water and quietly wondered what their new lives would be like.

Some immigrants that arrived in the United States were nervous. Learning new skills and a new language would be hard work. However, they were also excited about new opportunities.

Talk About It Why did the immigrants want to change? What changes would the immigrants need to make? Complete the sentences below.

> Immigrants wanted to change because _____.
>
> Immigrants would need to learn _____ and _____.

Your Turn Think of a change you would like to make. Tell a partner about how this change would help you.

Explaining To explain things clearly, we often use words that answer the question *how?* Some words that answer the question *how?* are *quietly, slowly, happily,* and *sadly.* These words often have *-ly* at the end.

Example: Luke studied his science lesson **carefully.**

The word *carefully* tells how Luke studied.

Circle the words that answer *how?* in the sentences below.

Mario eagerly waited for the steamship to arrive in the United States.

The line of immigrants waiting to enter the United States moved slowly.

Rosario sadly waved goodbye to her old friends.

Talk About It Use a word that answers the question *how?*

Tell a partner about something you did today. How did you do it?

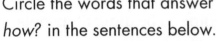

This morning, I _____.

Your Turn Look at the passage on page 145. Underline the word that answers the question *how?* Then use the word to write a sentence.

_____

_____

_____

ELA LC 1.2 Identify and correctly use verbs that are often misused (e.g., *lie/ lay, sit/ set, rise/ raise*), modifiers, and pronouns. (ELD LC I7)

Draw Conclusions We **draw conclusions** when we think about facts and details and make decisions about them. To explain our conclusions, we sometimes use words that answer the question *how?*

The family in this picture is getting off a steamship. This is a fact. We can draw the conclusion that the bags, carried by the father with the dark hat, are heavy. We draw that conclusion because his arm hangs low and he looks tired.

. . . .

Talk About It Look at the picture again. What else can you tell about the family? Tell a partner your conclusions.

> The mother carries the baby _____.
>
> The man in the back of the picture _____.
>
> The father walks slowly because _____.

. . . .

Your Turn Think about the passage you read on page 145. How do you think an immigrant may have felt coming to the United States by steamship?

Draw conclusions. Write two sentences to explain your conclusions.

An immigrant might have _____.

I think this because _____.

ELA R 2.4 Draw inferences, conclusions, or generalizations about text and support them with textual evidence and prior knowledge. (ELD R EA14)

147

Using *Who* and *Whom* *Who* and **whom** are pronouns.
They are used to tell about people or ask questions about people.
The words *who* and *whom* can tell about a person in a sentence.

Example: The immigrant (who) traveled here from Italy has a new job.
The new student, (whom) I met today, is from China.

The words *who* and *whom* can also be used to ask a question about a person.

Example: (Who) has changed the most this year?
To (whom) does this book belong?

Talk About It Read the sentences and underline
the person the words *who* or *whom* are referring to.

The passenger whom they met last night was the first to leave the steamship.

Many people who change themselves are looking for new opportunities.

My mother, who bought the tickets, did not complain.

Your Turn Finish each sentence. Use *who* or *whom* to complete the sentence.

_____ has traveled on a steamship?

To _____ does this suitcase belong?

ELA LC 1.2 Identify and correctly use verbs that are often misused (e.g., *lie/ lay, sit/ set, rise/ raise*), modifiers, and pronouns.
(ELD LC EA8)

Think, Talk, and Write

Improving Ourselves Think about how immigrants in the early 1900s tried to improve their lives. Talk with a partner about other ways people can make changes to improve their lives.

Can you improve your life by education?

Can you improve your life by moving?

Talk About It Review the vocabulary on page 144. Work with a partner to tell about each word. Which words will you use to write about a change you have made to improve yourself?

Produce Language Write about a change you have made to improve yourself. First complete the chart. Then write 5 to 6 sentences in your Weekly Concept Journal.

My change: _____

_____

Steps to changing: _____

_____

How I improved: _____

_____

Vocabulary words I can use: _____

_____

ELA W 2.1 Write narratives: a. Establish a plot, point of view, setting, and conflict. b. Show, rather than tell, the events of the story. (ELD W EA2)

149

Adventurers

 Who goes seeking adventure and why?

Everyday Adventures
How can we find adventure in ordinary events?

Technology and Adventurers
How does technology help adventurers reach new places?

Adventures in Space
What is life like for an astronaut?

Adventures Underground
How do we explore the center of Earth?

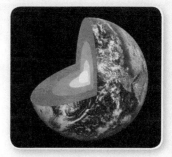

California Gold Rush
What adventures helped drive westward expansion?

Adventures

Everyday Adventures

Vocabulary

porch

soapsuds

attempt
clamped
feat
immensely
ordinary

How can we find adventure in ordinary events?

Adventure can happen even on an ordinary day. Sometimes exciting things happen at school or at home. As Luis would soon learn, a simple attempt to train a dog could end up being a very adventurous—and immensely messy—afternoon!

Read the passage together.
Then circle the vocabulary words.

Puppy Problems

Luis wanted his dog Hector to perform a new feat: to fetch the newspaper from the porch. The training wasn't going well. One rainy afternoon, Luis opened the door and said, "Fetch!" Instead of getting the newspaper, Hector ran outside and splashed through puddles. Hector came back into the house. He left muddy paw prints on the carpet and knocked over a lamp.

Luis decided to attempt to bathe Hector. But Hector wriggled from Luis's hands and ran back downstairs, leaving a trail of soapsuds. Luis ran after him. Hector was sitting in front of the open door with the newspaper clamped in his teeth!

"Oh sure, Hector! *Now* you get it!" Luis laughed.

Talk About It What were some of the everyday activities that Luis was doing that became an adventure? Complete the sentences below.

First, Luis was trying to _____.

Then, Luis tried to _____.

Your Turn Think about an adventure you have had on an ordinary day. Tell your partner your story.

ELA LS 2.1 Deliver narrative presentations: a. Establish a situation, plot, point of view, and setting with descriptive words and phrases. b. Show, rather than tell, the listener what happens. (ELD LS EA5)

153

Making Predictions We use words to make predictions, or tell what we think is going to happen in the future.

Example: The dog **will** learn to do more tricks.

When we make predictions, we use special verbs to tell what we think is going to happen.

Circle the verbs that are used to make predictions.

could	The dog could learn how to fetch other things.
might	The dog might be able to do another trick.
will	The dog will be able to fetch a newspaper again.

- -

Talk About It Look at the picture. What are your predictions?

Say two sentences that tell what you think is going to happen.

Luis will _____ .

Hector might _____ .

- -

Your Turn Look at the picture again. Write a sentence that tells what could happen.

_____

_____

_____

Character and Plot A story has a beginning, middle, and end, which form the **plot.** Often a **character** in a story will have a problem in the beginning. Sometimes when we know the problem, we can predict what is going to happen in the plot. In the middle, the problem reaches a climax. In the end the problem is resolved. This is the resolution.

Climax

Plot

Problem

Resolution

Talk About It Think about the story "Puppy Problems." What is the problem in that story? Complete the sentence with a partner.

Luis wants to _____ .

Your Turn Reread the story on page 153. Then write the problem, climax, and resolution of the story.

Problem _____

Climax _____

Resolution _____

ELA R 3.2 Identify the main problem or conflict of the plot and explain how it is resolved. (ELD R EA16)

155

Grammar

Contractions and Negatives In English, we can combine two words to make a shorter word. A **contraction** is a shortened form of two words. An apostrophe takes the place of letters taken out of the word to shorten it. Many contractions are formed by combining a verb and the word *not*. The circled words in the chart are contractions.

Example: The dog **isn't** too tired to do a trick.

Verb	Negative	Contraction
has	not	hasn't
can	not	can't
are	not	aren't
is	not	isn't
have	not	haven't

- -

Talk About It What are the contractions in these sentences?

Circle the contractions.

The dog can't fetch.

Hector hasn't fetched the newspaper yet.

Hector isn't clean.

- -

Your Turn Complete these sentences using contractions from the chart.

Anna _____ in my class at school.

We _____ go to the movie until we finish our homework.

 ELA LC 1.5 Spell roots, suffixes, prefixes, contractions, and syllable constructions correctly. (ELD LC EA7)

Think, Talk, and Write

Everyday Adventures Think about how Luis's ordinary activities became an adventure. Talk with a partner about an adventure you had on an ordinary day.

What could happen if the bird escaped?

What could happen on a windy day?

Talk About It Review the vocabulary on page 152. Work with a partner to tell about each word. Which words will you use to write about an ordinary day that became an adventure?

Produce Language Write a story about how an ordinary day became an adventure. First complete the chart. Then write 5 to 6 sentences in your Weekly Concept Journal.

The character: _____

_____

The ordinary day: _____

_____

The adventure: _____

_____

Vocabulary words I can use: _____

_____

ELA W 2.1 Write narratives: a. Establish a plot, point of view, setting, and conflict. b. Show, rather than tell, the events of the story. (ELD W I1)

157

Technology and Adventurers

Vocabulary

debris

ROV

operated
pressure
remotely
robotic
surface
technology

How does technology help adventurers reach new places?

Adventurers could not explore many places without tools to help them. For example, the deep sea is very cold and dark, and humans can't withstand heavy water pressure all around them. Luckily, robotic technology can help adventurers explore the deep sea safely.

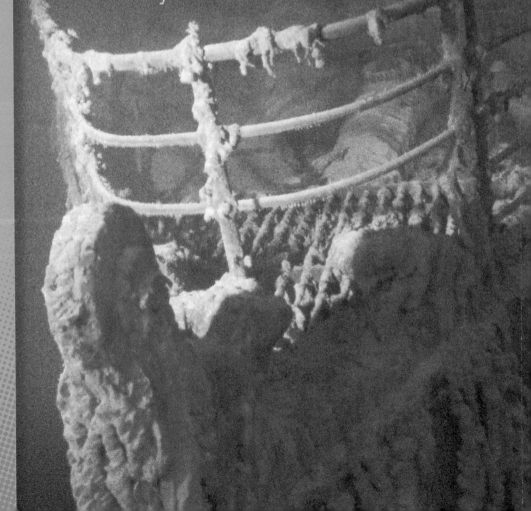

Read the passage together.
Then circle the vocabulary words.

Into the Deep

Hercules, a type of robot called a remotely operated vehicle (ROV), moved slowly down through the sea. At 12,500 feet, its lights shined on the debris of the sunken *Titanic*. The ROV's cameras sent back images to its human operator in a boat on the water's surface and to a TV channel. Hercules showed the world the first images of the sunken ship.

ROVs go where human explorers cannot. ROVs can handle underwater pressure and cold temperatures. They can record images of whatever explorers need to see. Some ROVs even have robotic arms that can grab objects and bring them back up to the surface!

Talk About It How does an ROV help adventurers reach new places? Complete the sentences below.

An ROV can go into the deep sea to _____.

Some ROVs have _____ that can _____.

Your Turn What other kinds of technology could help adventurers who want to explore the sea? Tell a partner about your ideas.

Draw Conclusions We use words to tell why we think something. We draw conclusions based on details and facts. Sometimes words can signal that someone is drawing his or her own conclusions. A person can draw a conclusion and explain it all in one sentence.

Example:

> In recent years, explorers have **probably** found new kinds of underwater animals **because** ROVs can go deeper than people can.

Circle the words that show a conclusion is being drawn.

seems as though, because	An ROV's robotic arm seems as though it would be useful for taking treasures off of sunken ships because a robotic arm can grab objects.
probably, because	Explorers are probably excited about ROVs because ROVs allow explorers to see deep into the sea.

Talk About It Say a sentence that draws a conclusion about ROVs. Be sure to add *because* to explain the fact that helped you draw the conclusion.

Your Turn Write a sentence that draws a conclusion about ROVs.

_____

_____

FORM & FUNCTION

Draw Conclusions How do you make a decision? How do you form an opinion? You do both of these things by thinking about facts and details. When you **draw conclusions,** you think about facts and details and decide something about them.

Example:

Facts and Details	Conclusion
Milo sat down in the canoe on the water. He picked up the oars and tried to move. Fifteen minutes passed. Milo had not moved any farther down the river.	Milo does not know how to paddle a canoe.

. . . .

Talk About It How do you know that the conclusion about Milo is correct? What are some facts or details that helped you draw this conclusion?

. . . .

Your Turn Read the paragraph and then answer the question.

They walked into the main hall. Each display showed how technology had helped people make airplanes. Ella looked up and saw an old plane made of cloth and wire hanging from the ceiling.

Where are Ella and her classmates?
Circle your answer.

in a grocery store

in a museum

in a library

ELA R 2.4 Draw inferences, conclusions, or generalizations about text and support them with textual evidence and prior knowledge. (ELD R EA14)

161

Grammar

Adjectives and Articles Adjectives are words that describe nouns and pronouns. The circled words are **adjectives.** The words with a box around them are **articles.** In English, there are three articles: *a, an,* and *the.*

What kind?	The (large) ship sank.
How many?	(Thirty) photos were taken by an ROV.
Which one?	The ROV took a picture of a (spotted) fish.

- -

Talk About It Read each sentence. Which words are adjectives? Which words are articles?

Circle each adjective and draw a box around each article.

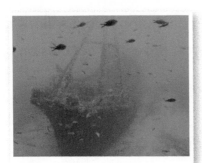

The ROV took many pictures of the sunken ship.

Three adventurers saw a strange animal.

- -

Your Turn Write a sentence about an adventure you would like to take. After you are finished, circle each adjective and draw a box around each article you used.

_____

_____

ELA LC 1.2 Identify and correctly use verbs that are often misused (e.g., *lie/lay, sit/set, rise/raise*), modifiers, and pronouns. (ELD LC 17)

Think, Talk, and Write

Technology and Adventurers Think about how the technology of the ROV helped adventurers reach new places. Talk with a partner about other explorations that may need technology.

How does the Rover help us explore Mars?

How does technology help us explore underwater?

Talk About It Review the vocabulary on page 158. Work with a partner to tell about each word. Which words will you use to write about an exploration that may need technology?

Produce Language Write about an exploration that may need technology. First complete the chart. Then write 5 to 6 sentences in your Weekly Concept Journal.

My exploration: _____

_____

My technology: _____

_____

How technology may help: _____

_____

Vocabulary words I can use: _____

_____

ELA W 2.3 Write research reports about important ideas, issues, or events by using the following guidelines: a. Frame questions that direct the investigation. b. Establish a controlling idea or topic. c. Develop the topic with simple facts, details, examples, and explanations. (ELD W I3)

163

Vocabulary

astronaut

space

space shuttle

space station

gravity

preparation

specific

What is life like for an astronaut?

Astronauts go on missions to explore space. Life in a space shuttle or on a space station is different than life on Earth. In space, even eating and sleeping can be an adventure.

Vocabulary in Context

Read the passage together.
Then circle the vocabulary words.

Living in Space

An astronaut can eat some of the same food in space that he or she eats on Earth. Fruit can be taken into space without special preparation. Other food must be prepared in specific ways. There are no refrigerators in space to keep food fresh. Astronauts add water to foods like spaghetti. When an astronaut eats, food needs to be held firmly. There is almost no gravity in space, so the food could float away in the air!

Gravity also affects how astronauts sleep. Astronauts on the space station and space shuttle usually sleep in sleeping bags. Astronauts must attach themselves to something so they stay in one place while sleeping.

· ·

Talk About It What is life like for an astronaut in space? Complete the sentences below.

> Gravity affects how astronauts _____
> and _____ .
>
> Astronauts eat _____ and prepare _____ .
>
> When they sleep, astronauts must _____ .

· ·

Your Turn How is life in space different than life on earth? Tell a partner.

ELA R 1.1 Read aloud narrative and expository text fluently and accurately and with appropriate pacing, intonation, and expression. (ELD R EA1)

165

Language Workshop FORM & FUNCTION

Asking Questions We ask questions to get information. Certain words are used to ask questions. When we ask questions, certain verbs such as *do, does, would,* and *might* follow the question word.

Example: How **does** an astronaut eat in space?

Circle the verb that follows the question word.

How	How might astronauts in space brush their teeth?
What	What do astronauts eat in space?
Why	Why would astronauts in space eat tortillas instead of bread?
When	When does the space shuttle take off?
Who	Who would want to go on a mission to explore Mars?

Talk About It Look at the picture. Say a sentence that asks a question. Use words from above to ask for specific information.

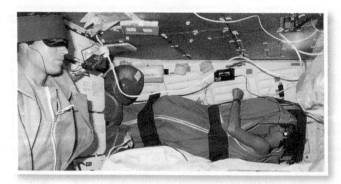

Your Turn Write a question about the astronauts in the picture above. Use words from the chart to ask for specific information.

_____

_____

ELA LS 1.1 Ask questions that seek information not already discussed. (ELD LS I1)

Author's Purpose Everything you read has a purpose. Some texts are written to inform, or give information. The article on page 165 was written to inform. Other texts are written to influence how you think about something. Sometimes a text is written to make you laugh. Asking questions about what you read will help you determine the **author's purpose.**

Astronauts must complete many tests before going into space. Doctors test the astronauts' hearing and eyesight. The astronauts also exercise their bodies to stay healthy.

Talk About It What questions can you ask about the text above? What is the author's purpose for writing the text above?

Complete the sentences below with a partner.

Why did _____?

The author's purpose is _____ because _____.

Your Turn What is the author's purpose for the following kinds of texts? Discuss with a partner.

1. an essay that asks for more money to be spent on missions to explore space

2. a fun story about traveling in space

3. an article that tells how astronauts get ready for a mission

ELA R 3.1 Identify and analyze the characteristics of poetry, drama, fiction, and nonfiction and explain the appropriateness of the literary forms chosen by an author for a specific purpose. (ELD R EA11)

This, That, These, Those English uses certain words to point to and identify nouns. These words are **this, that, these,** and **those.**

	Noun is close to speaker	**Noun is far from speaker**
Singular (only one)	I really like ⟨this⟩ book.	I really like ⟨that⟩ book.
Plural (more than one)	I really like ⟨these⟩ books.	I really like ⟨those⟩ books.

Talk About It Circle the words that point out the nouns in these sentences.

These posters are really colorful!   I really like this poster.

Your Turn Fill in the blanks using *this, that, these,* or *those.*

_____ telescope is closer to me than _____ telescope.

Please put _____ toys here and _____ toys over there.

ELA LC 1.2 Identify and correctly use verbs that are often misused (e.g., *lie/lay, sit/set, rise/raise*), modifiers, and pronouns. (ELD LC EA8)

Think, Talk, and Write

Adventures in Space Think about how different life is for astronauts when living in space. Talk with a partner about other ways life is different in space.

How do they
move in space?

How do they
eat in space?

Talk About It Review the vocabulary on page 164. Work with a partner to tell about each word. Which words will you use to write about the life of an astronaut?

Produce Language Write about an astronaut's experience in space. First complete the chart. Then write 5 to 6 sentences in your Weekly Concept Journal.

How my astronaut prepares: _____

_____

How my astronaut lives: _____

_____

What my astronaut works on: _____

_____

Vocabulary words I can use: _____

_____

ELA W 1.2 Create multiple-paragraph expository compositions: a. Establish a topic, important ideas, or events in sequence or chronological order. b. Provide details and transitional expressions that link one paragraph to another in a clear line of thought. c. Offer a concluding paragraph that summarizes important ideas and details. (ELD W I5)

169

Adventures Underground

Vocabulary

PICTURE IT!

armor

PICTURE IT!

iron

PICTURE IT!

planet

degrees
earthquakes
encases
layers

How do we explore the center of Earth?

Scientists have been exploring Earth for many years. They have dug into Earth. They have also studied earthquakes. Although there is still much that scientists don't know, they do know that our planet has layers.

inner core

outer core

lower mantle

upper mantle

crust

Read the passage together.
Then circle the vocabulary words.

Exploring the Center of Earth

Scientists have found that Earth is made of layers. The crust is the top layer. It acts almost like armor for the planet. It encases the other layers.

The next layer is the mantle. The heat in the mantle moves giant plates near Earth's surface, which sometimes causes earthquakes.

The final layer is the core, or center, of our planet. The outer core is made of hot liquid metal that is thousands of degrees. The inner core is solid iron that is about the size of our moon.

• •

Talk About It What information have scientists learned by exploring Earth? Complete the sentences below.

Earth is made of _____.

The heat in the mantle _____ and sometimes causes _____.

The outer core is _____ and the inner core is _____.

• •

Your Turn What dangers might scientists face if they were ever to travel to the center of Earth? Tell your partner.

🐻 **ELA R 1.1** Read aloud narrative and expository text fluently and accurately and with appropriate pacing, intonation, and expression. (ELD R I6)

171

Language Workshop FORM & FUNCTION

Sequencing We use words to show the order in which things happen.

Example: You would reach the mantle **before** you reach the core.

Sequence words can tell the order in which a number of actions took place.

Circle the words that tell the sequence.

before	Scientists would have to create a big, strong drill before they could dig to the center of Earth.
after	The drill would reach the mantle after digging through the crust.
while	The temperature would be very hot for the drill while it was in the liquid outer core.
finally	Finally, the drill would reach the solid inner core of Earth.

Talk About It Imagine you are taking a journey to the center of Earth. Which layers of Earth would you travel through, and in which order?

Tell a partner about your journey to the center of Earth. Use at least one sequence word in your description.

Your Turn Write a sentence that uses a sequence word from the chart above.

_____

_____

 ELA LS 1.4 Select a focus, organizational structure, and point of view for an oral presentation. (ELD LS I3)

Sequence Events in a story take place in a certain order. This order is called **sequence.** Clue words can help you figure out the sequence. Here are some clue words: *first, next, before, after, finally, at last.*

Circle the clue words in the paragraph below.

Scientists sometimes explore caves to learn about Earth. To explore a cave, a scientist must first gather her supplies. Next, she enters the cave with her team of people. The group then gathers information deep in the cave, such as water samples. Finally, the group makes the journey back out of the cave.

Talk About It Retell how scientists explore caves to learn about Earth. Complete the sentences below with a partner.

First, scientists _____ .

Next, the group _____ .

Finally, the group _____ .

Your Turn Look at the pictures below. Number them in the order that they would happen.

_____   _____   _____

ELA R 2.2 Analyze text that is organized in sequential or chronological order. (ELD R EA16)

173

Grammar

Comparative and Superlative Adjectives In English we use adjectives to compare two things. These are called **comparative adjectives.** We also use adjectives to compare three or more things. These adjectives are called **superlative adjectives.**

Adjective	Comparative Adjective	Superlative Adjective
big	bigger	biggest
deep	deeper	deepest
hot	hotter	hottest
beautiful	more beautiful	most beautiful
careful	less careful	least careful
good	better	best

Talk About It Which are the comparative and superlative adjectives in these sentences?

Circle them.

> Earth's other layers are thicker than the crust.
>
> The core is the thickest layer of all.
>
> The core is the hottest layer of Earth.

Your Turn Look at the picture of the sun and the planets. Use a comparative adjective to compare the size of the sun to the planets.

The sun is _____ than the planets.

 ELA LC 1.2 Identify and correctly use verbs that are often misused (e.g., *lie/lay, sit/set, rise/raise*), modifiers, and pronouns. (ELD LC EA8)

Think, Talk, and Write

Adventures Underground Think about the many layers between you and the center of Earth. Talk with a partner about the things you might see if you wanted to explore Earth's underground.

What might you see in this lagoon?

What might you see in this cave?

Talk About It Review the vocabulary on page 170. Work with a partner to tell about each word. Which words will you use to write a story about what happens on your journey to Earth's center?

Produce Language Write a story about what happens on your journey to Earth's center. First complete the chart. Then write 5 to 6 sentences in your Weekly Concept Journal.

My transportation: _____

_____

What I see: _____

_____

What dangers I face: _____

_____

Vocabulary words I can use: _____

_____

ELA W 2.1 Write narratives: a. Establish a plot, point of view, setting, and conflict. b. Show, rather than tell, the events of the story. (ELD W I1)

175

California Gold Rush

Vocabulary

PICTURE IT!

gold

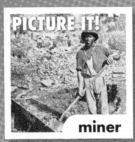

PICTURE IT!

miner

economic

general store

goods

independence

millionaire

services

What adventures helped drive westward expansion?

During the California Gold Rush, just about anyone could have an adventure. Many different people lived in the mining camps. Miners looked for gold. Other people had economic success by selling goods and services to the miners.

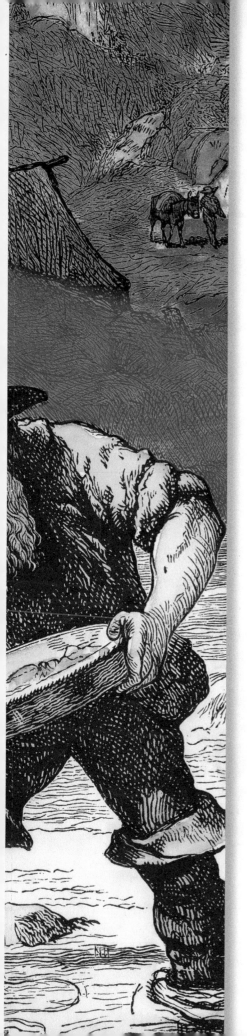

Vocabulary in Context

Read the passage together.
Then circle the vocabulary words.

Opportunities in Mining Camps

Not everyone who lived in California during the Gold Rush wanted to find gold. Some people saw an opportunity to make money in different ways. Sam Brannan owned a general store. By selling goods to miners, Brannan became California's first millionaire.

The few women who lived in mining camps made money by providing services for the miners. These services included washing clothes and making meals. A woman offering meal services would set up long wooden tables and benches. When the miners were finished working, they would pay her money to sit down to a hot meal. Many women achieved economic independence this way.

Talk About It How did people make money in mining camps? Complete the sentences below.

> Some women living in mining camps offered services, such as _____, to earn _____.
>
> Other people, such as Sam Brannan, earned money by _____.

Your Turn Pretend that you are living in a mining camp. What types of goods or services do you think you could offer? Tell your partner.

ELA R 1.1 Read aloud narrative and expository text fluently and accurately and with appropriate pacing, intonation, and expression. (ELD R I2)

177

Generalizing We use certain words to share an idea about several things or people. When we say something about all of them together, we are generalizing. When we generalize, we use words such as *all*, *most*, *usually*, and *few*, to make broad statements about a group.

Example: **Most women** in mining camps earned money by providing services.

Circle the words that show generalizing in the sentences below.

all	All miners wanted to find gold.
most, many	Many people made money by providing services to miners.
usually	Usually miners were men.
few, seldom	Few people can become millionaires.

Talk About It Look at the picture. Say a sentence that generalizes about the people in this mining camp. Use the words above to help you.

Your Turn Write a sentence that generalizes about the people in the mining camp picture.

_____

_____

ELA LS 1.5 Clarify and support spoken ideas with evidence and examples. (ELD LS EA3)

Comprehension Support

Generalize When you read, you are given ideas about several things or people. You can make a broad statement, or **generalization,** about all of them together. As you read, look for clue words that help you identify generalizations, such as *all*, *most*, *usually*, *never*, and *always*.

The California Gold Rush brought together people of different nations. Most of the people living in the mining towns came from different parts of the United States. There were some, though, who came from Asia and Europe.

Circle the clue word that signals a generalization in the text above.

. . . .

Talk About It What generalization can you make about the people living in the California mining towns?

Complete the sentence below with a partner.

> Most mining towns had _____ .

. . . .

Your Turn Read the paragraph below. Then write a generalization.

> Wagon trains heading west left from St. Louis, Missouri. The city's location on the Mississippi River made it easy to get to. The pioneers driving these wagon trains bought supplies from the St. Louis stores.

_____

_____

_____

ELA R 2.4 Draw inferences, conclusions, or generalizations about text and support them with textual evidence and prior knowledge. (ELD R EA14)

179

Adverbs Words that modify verbs or adjectives are called **adverbs.**
Adverbs generally answer one of four questions: *how? where? when?*
or *how much?* Many adverbs end with *-ly.* Examples of adverbs are circled
in the chart below.

The miner kept his gold nuggets (deep) in the mine.	Adverbs tell **where.**
We read a book (today) about Chinese immigrants who became gold miners.	Adverbs tell **when.**
Miners often shouted (excitedly) when they found gold.	Adverbs tell **how.**
The California Gold Rush was a (very) important event in California history.	Adverbs tell **how much.**

Talk About It Read each sentence.
Which words are adverbs?
Circle the adverbs.

> She quickly served food
> to the waiting miners.
>
> The hot food was very good.

Your Turn Write a sentence using an adverb from the chart above.

_____

_____

Think, Talk, and Write

California Gold Rush Think about what happened during the Gold Rush. Talk with a partner about ways people earned money.

Where did the miners sleep?

Who cared for the miners' horses?

Talk About It Review the vocabulary on page 176. Work with a partner to tell about each word. Which words will you use to write about adventures at a mining camp?

Produce Language Write about adventures at a mining camp. First complete the chart. Then write 5 to 6 sentences in your Weekly Concept Journal.

The adventure: _____

_____

What happened: _____

_____

What life was like at the mining camp: _____

_____

Vocabulary words I can use: _____

_____

ELA W 1.1 Create multiple-paragraph narrative compositions: a. Establish and develop a situation or plot. b. Describe the setting. c. Present an ending. (ELD W I5)

181

Get **Online!**
PearsonSuccessNet.com

Hear it!
See it!
Do it!

- Big Question Video
- Concept Talk Video
- Interactive Sound-
  Spelling Charts
- Picture It! Animation
- eBooks
- Grammar Jammer
- Online Journal

The Unexpected

What can we learn
from encounters with
the unexpected?

Unexpected Behavior
How can someone's unexpected behavior affect other people?

Humans' Effect on Nature
What unexpected effects can humans have on nature?

Unexpected Results of Our Actions
How can we learn from the results of our actions?

Safe Travel
How can unexpected encounters reveal hidden dangers?

Influences
What unexpected influence do we have on those around us?

The Unexpected

murals

sketched

emerge
political
public
revolution
unexpected

How can someone's unexpected behavior affect other people?

When someone does something unexpected, it can affect how other people think. It can inspire people. It can affect other people's actions. A Mexican artist named Diego Rivera was someone who did unexpected things and affected other people.

Vocabulary in Context

Read the passage together.
Then circle the vocabulary words.

DIEGO RIVERA: ARTIST FOR MEXICO

After the Mexican Revolution (1910–1920), the government paid artists to create murals. Murals were painted on the walls of public buildings. The murals were meant to show the history of Mexico and create pride in its people and culture.

Murals soon became one of the great art styles of the twentieth century. One of the greatest painters to emerge during this time was Diego Rivera.

Though he was paid to paint history, Rivera sketched the future. He inspired people to take political action for the love of their country. With his unexpected images, Rivera encouraged the common people of Mexico not to live in the past, but to rise to the challenges of the future.

· ·

Talk About It What was Diego Rivera's unexpected behavior? Complete the sentences below.

> The government expected Rivera to paint _____.
>
> Diego Rivera's murals encouraged _____.

· ·

Your Turn Think about what Diego Rivera's unexpected behavior meant to the people of Mexico. Tell a partner your thoughts.

ELA LS 1.8 Analyze media as sources for information, entertainment, persuasion, interpretation of events, and transmission of culture. (ELD LS I3)

185

Describing We can use words to describe characteristics. A characteristic is a quality that helps to identify a person or thing. Characteristics include what something looks like and what it does.

Thing	Characteristics	
mural	artwork, colorful, created for large space, can influence others	
painting	artwork, colorful, created for large and small spaces, can influence others	

Talk About It What are some other characteristics of murals and paintings? Complete the sentences below with a partner.

The characteristics of this mural are _____, _____, and _____.

The characteristics of this painting are _____, _____, and _____.

Your Turn Write a sentence about paintings and murals. Use words that describe the characteristics of each.

_____

_____

ELA LC 1.1 Identify and correctly use prepositional phrases, appositives, and independent and dependent clauses; use transitions and conjunctions to connect ideas. (ELD LC I8)

Comprehension Support

Classify and Categorize When we **classify,** or **categorize,** we group together several things that have similar characteristics. We tell how the parts of the group are alike. For example, a category might be *Unexpected Things.* Read the explanation below.

In some paintings, we see things that we expect. In these kinds of paintings, a person's face often looks so real it could be a photograph. Sometimes paintings show things that are unexpected. In these kinds of paintings, the person's face could be formed of sharp angles, or the eyes might not be in their usual places. The person's face might also be painted in bright colors.

Talk About It Classify each painting. Tell whether the subject of the painting is unexpected or expected.

Complete the sentences below with a partner.

This painting is unexpected because _____.

This painting is expected because _____.

Your Turn What is another thing that can be unexpected in a painting?

_____

_____

ELA R 2.4 Draw inferences, conclusions, or generalizations about text and support them with textual evidence and prior knowledge. (ELD R EA14)

187

Modifiers Some words add information about where, when, or how something is done. A **modifier** is a word or phrase that describes or adds detail to another word. A modifier works best when it is right next to the word it modifies. Look at the chart. Notice how a modifier changes a sentence.

Without a Modifier	With a Modifier
Diego Rivera is an artist.	Diego Rivera is a respected artist.
The Mexican Revolution was a period in history.	The Mexican Revolution was an important period in history.

Talk About It Read the sentences and circle the modifiers.

The colorful mural tells a story.

The plain building has a colorful mural.

Your Turn Look at the mural on one of the buildings. Write a sentence about what you see. Be sure to use a modifier to describe an image in the mural.

_____

_____

ELA LC 1.2 Identify and correctly use verbs that are often misused (e.g., *lie/lay, sit/set, rise/raise*), modifiers, and pronouns. (ELD LC I7)

Think, Talk, and Write

Unexpected Behavior Think about how Diego Rivera created the unexpected with his murals. Talk with a partner about other ways artists do unexpected things.

How is this painting by
Pablo Picasso unexpected?

How is this painting by
Keith Haring unexpected?

. . . .

Talk About It Review the vocabulary on page 184. Work with a partner to tell about each word. Which words will you use to write about how you might do something that is unexpected?

. . . .

Produce Language Write about something unexpected you might do. First complete the chart. Then write 5 to 6 sentences in your Weekly Concept Journal.

What I will do: _____

_____

Why it is unexpected: _____

_____

How it will affect people: _____

_____

Vocabulary words I can use: _____

_____

ELA W 1.1 Create multiple-paragraph narrative compositions: a. Establish and develop a situation or plot. b. Describe the setting. c. Present an ending. (ELD W I2)

189

Vocabulary

canopy

tundra

ecosystem
intentionally
lush
rare
scrawny
threat

What unexpected effects can humans have on nature?

Most often, the changes humans cause are done intentionally. But sometimes humans affect nature in ways they could not have expected. The effects humans have had on the Amazon rainforest were not expected.

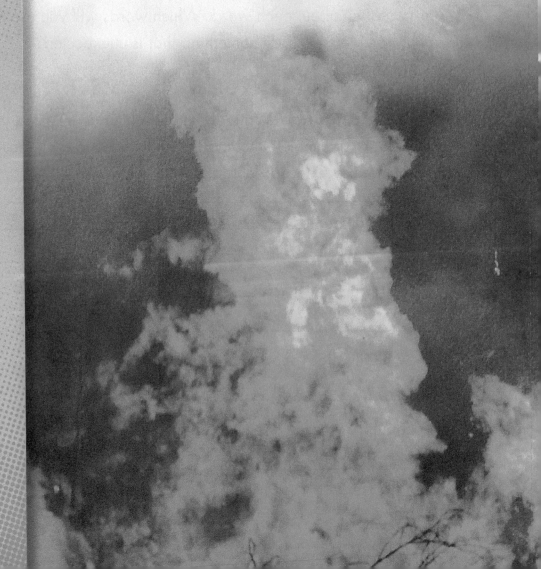

Vocabulary in Context

Read the passage together.
Then circle the vocabulary words.

Amazon Rainforest on Fire!

Before humans arrived, forest fires were rare in the Amazon. Now, fires are a great threat to the rainforest. Unlike the treeless plain of the Arctic tundra, the rainforest was once lush. Layers of plants provided food and habitats for thousands of species of animals and insects. Treetops formed a canopy, or covering, to shade the forest habitats.

Then people arrived to cut down trees to sell. Trees were also burned to make land for farming. These fires spread, destroying more of the forest. Small, scrawny trees began to replace the lost ones. But they are not enough to support the rainforest's ecosystem.

- -

Talk About It What unexpected effects have humans had on the rainforest? Complete the sentences below.

People have _____.

Fires were started to _____, but the fires spread and _____.

- -

Your Turn Think about what happens to the rainforest's ecosystem during a fire. What are the effects on the food and shelter provided by the rainforest? Tell a partner your thoughts.

ELA R 2.4 Draw inferences, conclusions, or generalizations about text and support them with textual evidence and prior knowledge. (ELD R EA14)

191

Language Workshop

Explaining We use words to explain things. Explaining is a way to help someone understand new information.

When we explain, we use declarative sentences to state facts and details. When we explain, we state the subject and then tell more about it.

Example: **Fires** are the greatest threat to the rainforest's massive ecosystem.

Read each declarative sentence. Underline the subject of the sentence.

Forest fires were a rare occurrence in the Amazon Rainforest before humans arrived.

Habitats are being destroyed by fires in the rainforest.

The rainforest may not survive.

Talk About It Say a declarative sentence that tells the condition of the rainforest today.

Your Turn Write a declarative sentence that explains why a healthy rainforest is important.

_____

_____

_____

_____

ELA LS 1.5 Clarify and support spoken ideas with evidence and examples. (ELD LS EA3)

Main Idea The most important idea about a topic is called the **main idea.** Each paragraph has a main idea. All the other sentences in the paragraph tell more about the main idea. These sentences support the main idea with facts and details. They are called supporting details.

Example:

> **Main Idea:** Fire is destroying the Amazon.

A main idea sentence is a declarative sentence. Supporting details are also declarative sentences.

· ·

Talk About It Read the passage about the Amazon on page 191. Use the sentences below to add details that support the main idea.

Complete the sentences below with a partner.

> Before humans arrived, the Amazon Rainforest was _____ .
>
> Now the rainforest's biggest threat is _____ .
>
> Humans can help stop the destruction by _____ .

· ·

Your Turn Read the paragraph below. Underline the main idea. What are the supporting details?

> The rainforest was once lush and green. Layers of plants provided food and habitats for thousands of species of animals and insects. Treetops formed a canopy, or covering, to shade the forest habitats.

ELA R 2.3 Discern main ideas and concepts presented in texts, identifying and assessing evidence that supports those ideas. (ELD R I11)

193

Grammar

Conjunctions Words or phrases of equal importance are often joined in sentences. The words that join phrases or lists of words are called **conjunctions.** Some common conjunctions are circled in the chart below.

Common Conjunctions	Example
and	The rainforest provides food (and) shelter.
or	We can choose to ignore the problem (or) try to do something about it.
but	Many people care about saving the rainforest, (but) don't know how they can help.

Talk About It Look at the two sentences. What do they have in common? What do both describe? What conjunction can be used to join the sentences?

The desert is hot.

The desert is dry.

Your Turn Combine the two sentences with the appropriate conjunction. Then write the new sentence on the line.

The rainforest is wet.

The desert is dry.

_____

_____

ELA LC 1.1 Identify and correctly use prepositional phrases, appositives, and independent and dependent clauses; use transitions and conjunctions to connect ideas. (ELD LC I8)

Think, Talk, and Write

Humans' Effect on Nature Think about how the Amazon Rainforest has been affected by humans. Talk with a partner about ways we affect nature unexpectedly in the United States.

How might we affect this redwood forest?

How might we affect Yellowstone Park?

Talk About It Review the vocabulary on page 190. Work with a partner to tell about each word. Which words will you use to write about how humans can have unexpected effects on nature?

Produce Language Write about how humans can have unexpected effects on nature in the United States. First complete the chart. Then write 5 to 6 sentences in your Weekly Concept Journal.

What may change: _____

_____

How it will change: _____

_____

How it could be stopped: _____

_____

Vocabulary words I can use: _____

_____

ELA W 2.3 Write research reports about important ideas, issues, or events by using the following guidelines: a. Frame questions that direct the investigation. b. Establish a controlling idea or topic. c. Develop the topic with simple facts, details, examples, and explanations. (ELD W EA6)

195

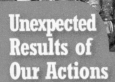

Unexpected Results of Our Actions

Vocabulary

temple

traveler

disguised

hospitality

mythology

precious

realm

results

How can we learn from the results of our actions?

All actions have results. It's important to think about the results of our actions. Usually our actions have good results. But sometimes the results are not what we expected. Many Greek myths are about the results of people's actions.

Read the passage together.
Then circle the vocabulary words.

KINDNESS REWARDED

Greek mythology tells the story of two gods named Zeus and Hermes. The gods decided to leave their realm and walk among the people to test their hospitality.

Zeus and Hermes disguised themselves as poor travelers. They asked for help at many wealthy villagers' homes. The people sent them away. The gods then asked a poor elderly couple for help. The husband and wife invited them into their home and treated them with great kindness.

Then Zeus and Hermes told the couple who they were. The gods thanked the couple by turning their home into a precious temple. Angry that everyone else had turned them away, Zeus and Hermes flooded the rest of the area, washing everything away.

Talk About It What were the results of people's actions? Complete the sentences below.

The elderly couple _____ and showed the travelers _____.

Because of their actions, Zeus and Hermes rewarded the couple by _____.

To punish the other villagers, the gods _____.

Your Turn What does the story teach about kindness? Share your ideas with a partner.

ELA R 1.1 Read aloud narrative and expository text fluently and accurately and with appropriate pacing, intonation, and expression. (ELD R I2)

197

Comparing and Contrasting We use words to tell how things or people are alike and different. We can use words that end in *-er* and *-est* to compare two or more things or people. Sometimes we use the words *most* and *more* to compare.

Example: The elderly couple were the **poorest** in the village, but they were **kinder** than the rest of the villagers to Zeus and Hermes.

Circle the words that show comparisons and contrasts.

-er words	The elderly couple were wiser than the wealthy villagers.
-est words	The elderly couple were the poorest people in the village.
more	The elderly couple were more respectful than the other villagers.
most	In many myths, gods have the most power.

Talk About It Look at the pictures of people volunteering. Say a sentence that compares the two pictures.

Your Turn Write a sentence that compares the two pictures. Use an *-er* or an *-est* word.

_____

_____

ELA LC 1.1 Identify and correctly use prepositional phrases, appositives, and independent and dependent clauses; use transitions and conjunctions to connect ideas. (ELD LC I8)

Compare and Contrast Writers often **compare and contrast** one thing to another thing. This helps the reader to see how the two things are the same or different.

The chart below compares the actions of the villagers to those of the poor elderly couple.

Villagers	Elderly Couple
turned the gods away	gave the gods food and shelter
were unfriendly and unkind	were friendly and kind
actions had bad results	actions had good results
shows that bad actions will have bad results	shows that good actions will have good results

Talk About It Compare and contrast the villagers and the elderly couple with a partner. Complete the sentences.

Unlike the villagers, the elderly couple _____.

The villagers were _____, but the elderly couple were _____.

Both the villagers' and the elderly couple's actions had _____.

Your Turn Write a sentence that compares or contrasts the villagers and the elderly couple. Use an *-er* or an *-est* word in your sentence.

_____

_____

ELA R 3.3 Contrast the actions, motives (e.g., loyalty, selfishness, conscientiousness), and appearances of characters in a work of fiction and discuss the importance of the contrasts to the plot or theme. (ELD R EA20)

199

Grammar

Commas Punctuation, such as **commas,** helps the reader understand the writer's meaning more clearly.

How Commas are Used	Example
to separate names or items in a series	The countryside had many hills, valleys, and rivers.
to set off a quotation	"Go away," said the villager to the traveler.
to show who is being spoken to or about	Wayfarer, we do not want you around here!

- -

Talk About It The sentences below are missing commas. Add commas to make the sentences correct.

Zeus said "You have been rewarded for your good actions."

Zeus was given food water and shelter.

- -

Your Turn Read the sentences below. Put commas where they belong.

"We are tired hungry and poor" said the travelers.

"I have meat bread and milk" said the elderly woman. "Eat!"

ELA G4 LC 1.4 Use parentheses, commas in direct quotations, and apostrophes in the possessive case of nouns and in contractions. (ELD LC EA7)

Think, Talk, and Write

Unexpected Results of Our Actions Think about how the elderly couple received an unexpected reward for their kindness to Zeus and Hermes. Talk with a partner about a time when your actions resulted in something good.

What results can recycling have?

What results can helping people have?

· ·

Talk About It Review the vocabulary on page 196. Work with a partner to tell about each word. Which words will you use to write about one of your actions that you learned from?

· ·

Produce Language Write about what you learned from the result of one of your actions. First complete the chart. Then write 5 to 6 sentences in your Weekly Concept Journal.

My action: _____

_____

The result: _____

_____

What I learned: _____

_____

Vocabulary words I can use: _____

_____

ELA W 2.1 Write narratives: a. Establish a plot, point of view, setting, and conflict. b. Show, rather than tell, the events of the story. (ELD W I4)

201

Vocabulary

explosion

harbor

hull

iceberg

cruised

unsinkable

How can unexpected encounters reveal hidden dangers?

An unexpected encounter is one that no one thinks will happen. Unexpected encounters, such as the *Titanic*'s hitting an iceberg, can sometimes create dangers.

Vocabulary in Context

Read the passage together.
Then circle the vocabulary words.

THE SINKING OF TITANIC

Titanic was one of the world's grandest ships. It was considered to be unsinkable. On April 10, 1912, it cruised out of a harbor in England. Around midnight four days later, the ship ran into a huge iceberg.

The iceberg damaged the hull of *Titanic*. Water flowed into the lower levels of the ship. The crash also caused a large explosion in the engine room. Soon, the unsinkable *Titanic* was sinking.

The passengers tried to get off the ship. Some used small boats to get away, but there were not enough boats for everyone. Many jumped into the cold water. Most passengers in the water did not survive. Only 705 of the 2,227 people aboard were rescued.

· ·

Talk About It What unexpected encounter did *Titanic* have? Complete the sentences below.

> *Titanic*, a grand ship, was thought to be _____,
> but the ship _____ and began to sink.
>
> As a result of *Titanic's* unexpected encounter with
> the iceberg, _____ .

· ·

Your Turn Think of an unexpected encounter you have experienced. How did this encounter affect you? Share your experience with a partner.

Classifying When we define something, we tell about its characteristics. We also tell how it relates to other things. We use certain words to classify, or to put things into groups based on similar characteristics.

Example: What happened to the cruise ship *Titanic* was one **kind** of dangerous encounter. Another **type** of dangerous encounter was when airplane pilot Amelia Earhart disappeared.

Circle the words that help you classify.

kind	A cruise ship is one kind of boat.
type	A speed boat is another type of boat.
in common	One thing all boats have in common is that they travel on water.

. . . .

Talk About It Say a sentence that classifies boats.

Complete the sentences with a partner.

One kind of boat is _____.

Another type of boat is _____.

One thing all boats have in common is that they _____.

. . . .

Your Turn Write two sentences that classify ways people can travel.

_____

_____

Classify and Categorize When we **classify,** we group together several things that have something in common. When we **categorize,** we tell how the parts of the group are alike.

For example, a category might be *Things That Fly.* Things that have this characteristic include birds and airplanes.

Talk About It Danger exists in almost everyone's daily life. Maybe you do not even think of things such as crossing a busy street as dangers. Think of an unexpected danger you could encounter. Then discuss some ways to stay safe.

Complete the sentences below with your partner.

> One kind of dangerous situation is _____.
>
> Another kind is _____.
>
> To stay safe, we can _____.

Your Turn Look at the list below. To what category do these things belong?

helmet   seat belt   airbags

Category: _____

ELA R 2.4 Draw inferences, conclusions, or generalizations about text and support them with textual evidence and prior knowledge. (ELD R EA16)

205

Grammar

Quotations and Quotation Marks When you write the exact words that a person or character said, you put **quotation marks** before and after the words. Quotation marks let the reader know that these are the words actually spoken by a person or character. The words inside quotation marks are called **quotations.**

Examples: "The ship is sinking," said a passenger.
              "We hit an iceberg!" yelled a sailor.

- -

Talk About It Where do the quotation marks belong in the following sentences?

Add quotation marks to the sentences.

This ship is unsinkable, said the captain.

We have to save the people in the water! the sailor screamed.

- -

Your Turn Ask a partner to tell you a sentence about the *Titanic*. Then complete the sentence below. Add quotation marks to your sentence.

My partner said, _____

_____

ELA LC 1.3 Use a colon to separate hours and minutes and to introduce a list; use quotation marks around the exact words of a speaker and titles of poems, songs, short stories, and so forth. (ELD LC EA7)

Think, Talk, and Write

Safe Travel Think about how the people on the *Titanic* felt as the ship sank. Talk with a partner about how you can prepare for the unexpected when traveling.

Can a seat belt keep you safe?

Can following the rules of the road keep you safe?

- -

Talk About It Review the vocabulary on page 202. Work with a partner to tell about each word. Which words will you use to write about how you can prepare for the unexpected when you travel?

- -

Produce Language Write about how you can prepare for the unexpected when you travel. First complete the chart. Then write 5 to 6 sentences in your Weekly Concept Journal.

My destination: _____

_____

What to bring: _____

_____

How I can prepare: _____

_____

Vocabulary words I can use: _____

_____

ELA W 2.3 Write research reports about important ideas, issues, or events by using the following guidelines: a. Frame questions that direct the investigation. b. Establish a controlling idea or topic. c. Develop the topic with simple facts, details, examples, and explanations (ELD W I3)

PICTURE IT!

clarinet

PICTURE IT!

fire escape

delighted
influence
nighttime
recital
secondhand

What unexpected influence do we have on those around us?

When a person causes change in someone's life, they have influenced another person. All people can influence others. Often people discover that they have influenced someone's life in an unexpected or surprising way.

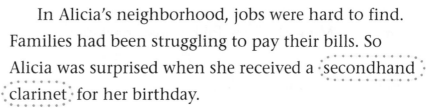

Read the passage together.
Then circle the vocabulary words.

More Than a Song

In Alicia's neighborhood, jobs were hard to find. Families had been struggling to pay their bills. So Alicia was surprised when she received a (secondhand clarinet) for her birthday.

Alicia sat on the fire escape at night. It was a good place to practice her clarinet. Alicia's elderly neighbor, Ms. Rogers, listened by the window. Alicia's songs made the lonely woman happy. Ms. Rogers looked forward to the nighttime concerts.

One day, Ms. Rogers made a dress for Alicia to thank her for the gift of music. Alicia was surprised and delighted to learn that someone had been listening all that time. Alicia invited Ms. Rogers to her first clarinet recital, where she wore her new dress on stage and played beautifully.

Talk About It How did Alicia unexpectedly influence Ms. Rogers? Complete the sentences below.

> Alicia received a _____ for her birthday
> and she _____ .
>
> Alicia's music made Ms. Rogers _____ ,
> so Ms. Rogers _____ .

Your Turn Think of a time when something you did made someone else happy. Tell a partner about your experience.

Literary Analysis We can use descriptive words when we write to create a picture of a person, place, or thing in our reader's minds. The author of the story about Alicia and Ms. Rogers uses descriptive words to help the reader know more about the two characters.

Example: My **elderly** neighbor lives next door.

Elderly describes the neighbor.

Circle the descriptive words in the sentences below.

Words with -ly	Alicia's elderly neighbor listened by the open window.
Words with -ful	Her joyful songs made the lonely woman grateful.
Compound words	Alicia received a secondhand clarinet. She was hardworking.

- -

Talk About It Look at the picture. Say sentences using descriptive language.

- -

Your Turn Look at the picture. Write a sentence that uses descriptive language.

_____

_____

ELA LC 1.2 Identify and correctly use verbs that are often misused (e.g., *lie/lay, sit/set, rise/raise*), modifiers, and pronouns.
(ELD LC I8)

Theme and Setting The central message or lesson the writer wants the reader to gain from a story is called the **theme.** The **setting** is where and when the story takes place.

Write the setting underneath each picture.

_____   _____

. . . .

Talk About It Why is it important to know when and where a story takes place? Look at the two different settings above. Use descriptive language to describe the two settings. How would the story be different for each of those settings? Complete the sentences with a partner.

> The first setting is _____.
>
> The other setting is _____.
>
> The two stories would be different because _____.

. . . .

Your Turn Reread the story "More Than a Song." Write the answers that best describe the story below.

The theme for this story is _____.

The setting for this story is _____.

ELA R 3.4 Understand that *theme* refers to the meaning or moral of a selection and recognize themes (whether implied or stated directly) in sample works. (ELD R EA21)

211

Colon A **colon** can be used to introduce a list of items. A colon may introduce a list of things, people, or places. A colon may also be used to introduce an explanation or a definition of something. The colons are circled in the chart below.

to introduce a list	These are some important things in Alicia's life: music, friends, and family.
	Ms. Rogers used three things to make Alicia's dress: material, thread, and a needle.
to introduce an explanation or definition	The Great Depression: a crisis that occurred in the 1920s and 1930s.

Talk About It Where is the colon in the sentence below? Circle the colon.

> To play the clarinet, Alicia had to learn three things: how to read music, how to hold the clarinet, and how to blow into the clarinet just right.

Your Turn Place a colon and commas in each sentence below.

The girl had several hobbies reading knitting and playing the clarinet.

The elderly woman's apartment had few furnishings a bed a table and some photos on the wall.

ELA LC 1.3 Use a colon to separate hours and minutes and to introduce a list; use quotation marks around the exact words of a speaker and titles of poems, songs, short stories, and so forth. (ELD LC EA7)

Think, Talk, and Write

Influences Think about how Alicia's music made her elderly neighbor happy. Talk with a partner about the people you may influence unexpectedly.

How do you influence your siblings?

How do you influence your friends?

· ·

Talk About It Review the vocabulary on page 208. Work with a partner to tell about each word. Which words will you use to write about how someone has influenced you unexpectedly?

· ·

Produce Language Write about how someone has influenced you unexpectedly. First complete the chart. Then write 5 to 6 sentences in your Weekly Concept Journal.

Who influenced me: _____

_____

How he or she influenced me: _____

_____

What has changed: _____

_____

Vocabulary words I can use: _____

_____

ELA W 1.1 Create multiple-paragraph narrative compositions: a. Establish and develop a situation or plot. b. Describe the setting. c. Present an ending. (ELD W I2)

213

Glossary

How to Use This Glossary

This glossary can help you understand and pronounce some of the words in this book. The words at the top of each page show the first and last words on the page. The pronunciation key is on page 215. Remember, if you can't find the word you are looking for, ask for help or check a dictionary.

The entry word is in dark type. It shows how the word is spelled.

The pronunciation is in parentheses. It also shows which syllables are stressed.

Part-of-speech labels show the function of the word.

adapt (ə dapt′), *v.* to change your behavior or ideas to fit a new situation

Aa

accurate (ak′yər it), *ADJ.* correct and true

achieved (ə chēv′ed), *v.* succeeded in doing something good

adapt (ə dapt′), *v.* to change your behavior or ideas to fit a new situation

adaptation (ad′ap tā′shən), *N.* the process of changing behavior for a new situation

American Revolution (ə mer′ə kən rev′ə lü′shən), *N.* a war fought many years ago between the American colonies and Great Britain

appreciate (ə prē′shē āt), *v.* to understand and enjoy the good qualities of something

appreciation (ə prē′shə ā′shən), *N.* the feeling of being thankful for something

armor (är′mər), *N.* metal or leather clothing that protects the body

assessment (ə ses′mənt), *N.* a test

assignment (ə sīn′mənt), *N.* a piece of work that is given to someone to complete

assistance (ə sis′təns), *N.* help or support

astonished (ə ston′ish ed), *ADJ.* surprised

astronaut (as′trə nȯt), *N.* someone who travels into space

attempt (ə tempt′), *N.* to try to do something

Bb

baggage (bag′ij), *N.* the bags used when traveling

brave (brāv), *ADJ.* able to deal well with or face a difficult or dangerous situation

Cc

camped (kamp ed), *v.* slept outdoors

campfire (kamp′fīr′), *N.* a small outdoor fire

canopy (kan′ə pē), *N.* the thick top leaves of trees that provide shelter for animals

challenge (chal′enj), *N.* something that tests your skill or ability

civilization (siv′ə lə zā′shən), *N.* a society that is well organized and developed

clamped (klamp ed), *v.* held something so tightly that it did not move

clarinet (klar′ə net′), *N.* a wooden musical instrument shaped like a long tube

cloak (klōk), *N.* a warm piece of clothing that is worn like a coat

collapsed (kə laps′ed), *v.* fell down

combination (kom′bə nā′shən), *N.* two or more different things that are put together

competition (kom′pə tish′ən), *N.* a contest in which people try to win a prize

concealed (kən sēl′ ed), *v.* hid something

conditions (kən dish′əns), N. situations that someone or something is in

confidence (kon′fə dəns), N. the belief that you have the ability to do things well

conservation (kon′sər vā′shən), N. the protection of animals, plants, or forests

contribute (kən trib′yüt), V. to give or offer money, help, or ideas

cornet (kôr net′), N. a small musical instrument that you blow into

courageously (kə rā′jəs ly), ADV. acting bravely when there is danger

critical (krit′ə kəl), ADJ. negative, or showing problems with something

cruised (krüzed), V. sailed along slowly

Dd

debris (də brē′), N. all the pieces that are left behind after something has been damaged

defense (di fens′), N. protection

degrees (di grēs′), N. a unit for measuring temperature

delighted (di li′tid), ADJ. happy and pleased

destructive (di struk′tiv), ADJ. causing damage

devastation (dev′ə stā′shən), N. very bad damage or complete destruction

device (di vīs′), N. a machine or other small object that does a special job

dinosaur (dī′nə sôr), N. a very large animal that lived long ago and no longer exists

disguised (dis gīz′ed), V. changed your appearance or voice

driftwood (drift′wůd′), N. wood floating in the ocean or left on the shore

Ee

earthquakes (ėrth′kwāks′), N. a sudden shaking of the earth's surface

economic (ē′kə nom′ik), ADJ. relating to money

ecosystem (ē′kōsis′təm), N. all the animals and plants in a certain area and how they work together

educated (ej′ə kā′tid), ADJ. having knowledge as a result of study

embryo (em′brē ō), N. an animal or human that has not yet been born

emerge (i merj′), V. to appear or come out

emergency (i mer′jən sē), N. something unexpected and dangerous

enables (en ā′bəls), V. makes able to do something

encases (en kās′ es), V. covers or surrounds something completely

encounter (en koun′tər), V. to experience something difficult

encouraged (en kėr′ij ed), V. persuaded someone to do something

endangered (en dān′jərd), ADJ. in danger of not surviving

enslaved (en slāv′ ed), V. forced by someone to work for little or no pay

entertain (en′tər tān′), V. to do something that interests and amuses people

a in hat	ėr in term	ô in order	ch in child	ə = a in about
ā in age	i in it	oi in oil	ng in long	ə = e in taken
â in care	ī in ice	ou in out	sh in she	ə = i in pencil
ä in far	o in hot	u in cup	th in thin	ə = o in lemon
e in let	ō in open	ů in put	ᴛʜ in then	ə = u in circus
ē in equal	ȯ in all	ü in rule	zh in measure	

environment • intellectual

environment (en vī′rən mənt), N. the air, water, and land where plants and animals live

explosion (ek splō′zhən), N. an event when something bursts into tiny pieces

extraordinary (ek strôr′də ner′ē), ADJ. very unusual, great, or impressive

eyeglasses (ī′glas′əz), N. clear glass in frames used to help someone see well

Ff

fabulous (fab′yə ləs), ADJ. extremely good

feat (fēt), N. something that is difficult to do

fire escape (fīr e skāp′), N. metal stairs on the outside of a building

firefighter (fīr′fī′tər), N. a member of the fire department who helps stop fires

fossil (fos′əl), N. part of an animal or plant that lived millions of years ago

freedom (frē′dəm), N. the right to do what you want

Gg

gadgets (gaj′its), N. small tools or machines that makes a job easier

general store (jen′ər əl stôr), N. a small town store that sells many different items

generations (jen′ə rā′shəns), N. people in a society who about the same age

glimmer (glim′ər), N. a small amount of

gnawed (nȯ ed), V. bit or chewed on

gold (gōld), N. a soft yellow metal

goods (gu̇dz), N. items that are sold

gorilla (gə ril′ə), N. the largest type of ape

gratitude (grat′ə tüd), N. the feeling of being grateful

gravity (grav′ə tē), N. the force that makes objects fall to the ground

gymnast (jim′nast), N. someone who does gymnastics

Hh

habitat (hab′ə tat), N. the environment in which a plant or animal lives

hammocks (ham′əks), N. large pieces of material hanging between two trees or poles that you can sleep or rest on

harbor (här′bər), N. an area of water next to the land, where ships can stay safely

heroine (her′ō ən), N. a female hero

hesitation (hez′ə tā′shən), N. the action of waiting before doing something

honest (on′ist), ADJ. truthful

hospitality (hos′pə tal′ə tē), N. friendly behavior toward visitors or guests

hull (hul), N. the main body of a ship

Ii

iceberg (is′bėrg′), N. a very large piece of ice floating in the ocean

imagination (i maj′ə nā′shən), N. the ideas that are formed in your mind

immensely (i mens′lē), ADV. very much

immigrants (im′ə grənts), N. people who enter a country other than their own to live there

impressed (im pres′ ed), V. made someone like something that you have done

independence (in′di pen′dəns), N. the freedom and ability to make decisions

influence (in′flü əns), V. to have an effect on or change something a person does

inspecting (in spekt′ ing), V. looking over something very carefully

inspired (in spīr′ ed), V. encouraged someone to do or produce something

intellectual (in′tə lek′chü əl), ADJ. related to the ability to think or understand ideas and information

intentionally (in ten′shə nəlē), *ADV.* deliberately; on purpose

investigation (in ves′tə gā′shən), *N.* an attempt to find out the reasons for something, such as a crime

iron (ī′ən), *N.* a common hard metal that is used to make steel

island (ī′lənd), *N.* a piece of land with water all around it

Jj

jazz (jaz), *N.* a type of popular music that is played with brass musical instruments

joints (joints), *N.* a place where two body parts are joined

Ll

landscape (land′skāp), *N.* a view of an area of land, including hills, forests, and fields

language (lang′gwij), *N.* a system of words used by people to talk with each other

layers (lā′ərs), *N.* two or more coverings of a surface on top of each other

legal (lē′gəl), *ADJ.* allowed by law

lightning rod (līt′ning rod), *N.* a tall pole that protects a building from lightning

lush (lush), *ADJ.* having lots of very green and healthy plants or leaves

Mm

memorize (mem′ə riz′), *V.* to learn and remember information

menacing (men′is′ing), *ADJ.* making you expect something dangerous

midst (midst), *N.* the middle of something

millionaire (mil′yə nâr′), *N.* someone who has at least one million dollars

miner (mī′ər), *N.* someone whose job it is to dig the earth and collect minerals

miniature (min′ē ə chúr), *ADJ.* much smaller than the usual thing of its type

model (mod′l), *N.* a smaller copy of something, such as a building or a city

moral (môr′əl), *ADJ.* knowing what is right and wrong

murals (myür′əls), *N.* large paintings that are painted on a wall

mythology (mi thol′ə jē), *N.* a set of stories that are meant to explain different events

Nn

narrow (nar′ō), *ADJ.* only measuring a small distance from side to side

nature (nā′chər), *N.* everything in the world that is not made by humans

nervous (nèr′vəs), *ADJ.* worried or frightened

newspaper (nüz′pā′pər), *N.* large sheets of paper containing news

nighttime (nīt′tīm′), *N.* the time during the night when the sky is dark

Oo

occasion (ə kā′zhən), *N.* a certain time when something happens

operated (op′ə rāt′ed), *V.* made a machine work

opportunities (op′ər tü′nə tēs), *N.* times when it is possible to do something

ordinary (ôrd′n er′ē), *ADJ.* very plain

overcome (ō′vər kum′), *V.* to succeed in solving a problem or challenging situation

oxen (ok′sən), *N.* two or more of a kind of male cow

Pp

paleontologists (pā′lē on tol′ə jists), *N.* people who study fossils

passengers (pas′n jərs), N. people traveling in a car, airplane, or boat but not driving

personal (pėr′sə nəl), ADJ. belonging to one person only

photographer (fə tog′rə fər), N. someone who takes pictures with a camera

physical (fiz′ə kəl), ADJ. relating to the body

pioneer (pī′ə nir′), N. one of the first people to live in a new or unknown place

planet (plan′it), N. a very large round object in space that moves around a star

plenty (plen′tē), N. enough of something

political (pə lit′ə kəl), ADJ. relating to the government

porch (porch), N. a structure built onto a house, with a floor and roof but no walls

possession (pə zesh′ən), N. something that belongs to you

precious (presh′əs), ADJ. valuable and important

preparation (prep′ə rā′shən), N. the process of having something ready in advance

preserve (pri zėrv′), V. to save something

pressure (presh′ər), N. the force of a gas or liquid in a container

previous (prē′vē əs), ADJ. happening before a time or event

print (print), V. to put words, numbers, or pictures on paper, using a machine

printing press (prin′ting pres), N. a machine that is used to print

promote (prə mōt′), V. to help something develop and be successful

protect (prə tekt′), V. to keep someone or something safe from harm or damage

public (pub′lik), ADJ. open for everyone's use

published (pub′lished), V. arranged for a written work to be printed and sold

Qq

quicker (kwik′er), ADJ. faster

Rr

rare (râr), ADJ. not seen or found very often

ravine (rə vēn), N. a deep and narrow area between hills or mountains

realm (relm), N. a general area of knowledge, activity, or thought

recital (re sī′tl), N. a public performance of a piece of music, dance, or poetry

remotely (ri mōt′ ly), ADV. from far away

representatives (rep′ri zen′tə tivs), N. people chosen to speak or make decisions

rescue (res′kyü), V. to save someone or something from harm or danger

resourceful (ri sôrs′fəl), ADJ. good at finding ways to deal with problems

results (ri zults′), N. things that happen because of other things that happened

revolution (rev′ə lü′shən), N. a time when people change a government by force

risks (risks), N. the chance that something bad may happen

roam (rōm), V. to walk or travel around

robotic (rō bot′ik), ADJ. describing something that works by remote control

ROV (Remotely Operated Vehicle), N. a machine that moves with remote controls

Ss

scarce (skârs), ADJ. hard to get

scrawny (skrò′nē), ADJ. very thin and weak

seamstress (sēm′stris), N. a woman whose job is to make and sew clothes

secondhand (sek′ənd hand′), ADJ. not new

seeking (sēk′ ing), V. trying to find or get something

serious (sir′ē əs), ADJ. very interested or involved in something

services (sèr′vises), N. the duties that are done for someone, such as cleaning or cooking

situations (sich′ü ā′shəns), N. the things that happen at a certain time and place

skeleton (skel′e tən), N. all the bones in a human or animal body

sketched (sketched) , V. drew quickly

skyscraper (skī′skrā′pər), N. a tall building

soapsuds (sōp′sudz′), N. bubbles

soared (sôred), V. flew high into the sky

soloist (sō′lō ist), N. a musician who plays music or sings alone

space (spās), N. the area beyond the Earth including the stars and other planets

space shuttle (spās shut′l), N. a vehicle for carrying people into space

space station (spās stā′shən), N. a type of building that stays in space

specialize (spesh′ə līz), V. use for one purpose

specific (spi sf′ik), ADJ. exact

spectacular (spek tak′yə lər), ADJ. very impressive or beautiful

station (stā′shən), N. a building or place that is a center for a type of activity

steamship (stēm′ship′), N. a large boat that carries passengers

sternly (stèrn′ly), ADV. done in a serious way

strict (strict), ADJ. demanding that rules be followed

style (stīl), N. a way of doing something

suddenly (sud′n ly), ADV. quickly

superiors (sə pir′ē ərs), N. people having a higher position than others

supplies (sə plīs′), N. things that you need for daily life

surface (sèr′fis), N. the top layer

survive (sər vīv′), V. to continue to live

Tt

talented (tal′ən tid), ADJ. having a natural ability or skill to do something well

technology (tek nol′ə jē), N. the knowledge and tools used in science

temple (tem′pəl), N. a building where people go to practice religion

threat (thret), N. a chance of possible danger

tornado (tôr nā′dō), N. a very violent and dangerous storm

trail (trāl), N. a path across open country

traveler (trav′ə lər), N. someone who moves around from place to place

trumpet (trum′pit), N. a musical instrument that is a long, bent metal tube

truth (truth), N. the correct facts

tundra (tun′drə), N. the large flat areas of land in the northern parts of the world

Uu

unexpected (un′ek spek′tid), ADJ. surprising

unique (yü nēk′), ADJ. one of a kind

unsinkable (un singk′ə bəl), ADJ. not able to be sunk, or pushed underwater

uproot (up rüt′), V. to pull a whole tree or plant completely out of the ground

Ww

wagon (wag′ən), N. a vehicle with four wheels, pulled by horses or oxen

wilderness (wil′dər nis), N. an area of land that has never been farmed or built on

Standards

CALIFORNIA

ENGLISH-LANGUAGE ARTS

Reading Standards

1.0 Word Analysis, Fluency, and Systematic Vocabulary Development

Students use their knowledge of word origins and word relationships, as well as historical and literary context clues, to determine the meaning of specialized vocabulary and to understand the precise meaning of grade-level-appropriate words.

Word Recognition

1.1 Read aloud narrative and expository text fluently and accurately and with appropriate pacing, intonation, and expression.

Vocabulary and Concept Development

1.2 Use word origins to determine the meaning of unknown words.

1.3 Understand and explain frequently used synonyms, antonyms, and homographs.

1.4 Know abstract, derived roots and affixes from Greek and Latin and use this knowledge to analyze the meaning of complex words (e.g., *controversial*).

1.5 Understand and explain the figurative and metaphorical use of words in context.

2.0 Reading Comprehension (Focus on Informational Materials)

Students read and understand grade-level-appropriate material. They describe and connect the essential ideas, arguments, and perspectives of the text by using their knowledge of text structure, organization, and purpose. The selections in *Recommended Literature, Kindergarten Through Grade Twelve* illustrate the quality and complexity of the materials to be read by students. In addition, by grade eight, students read one million words annually on their own, including a good representation of grade-level-appropriate narrative and expository text (e.g., classic and contemporary literature, magazines, newspapers, online information). In grade five, students make progress toward this goal.

Structural Features of Informational Materials

2.1 Understand how text features (e.g., format, graphics, sequence, diagrams, illustrations, charts, maps) make information accessible and usable.

2.2 Analyze text that is organized in sequential or chronological order.

Comprehension and Analysis of Grade-Level-Appropriate Text

2.3 Discern main ideas and concepts presented in texts, identifying and assessing evidence that supports those ideas.

2.4 Draw inferences, conclusions, or generalizations about text and support them with textual evidence and prior knowledge.

Expository Critique

2.5 Distinguish facts, supported inferences, and opinions in text.

3.0 Literary Response and Analysis

Students read and respond to historically or culturally significant works of literature. They begin to find ways to clarify the ideas and make connections between literary works. The selections in *Recommended Literature, Kindergarten Through Grade Twelve* illustrate the quality and complexity of the materials to be read by students.

Structural Features of Literature

3.1 Identify and analyze the characteristics of poetry, drama, fiction, and nonfiction and explain the appropriateness of the literary forms chosen by an author for a specific purpose.

Narrative Analysis of Grade-Level-Appropriate Text

3.2 Identify the main problem or conflict of the plot and explain how it is resolved.

3.3 Contrast the actions, motives (e.g., loyalty, selfishness, conscientiousness), and appearances of characters in a work of fiction and discuss the importance of the contrasts to the plot or theme.

3.4 Understand that *theme* refers to the meaning or moral of a selection and recognize themes (whether implied or stated directly) in sample works.

3.5 Describe the function and effect of common literary devices (e.g., imagery, metaphor, symbolism).

Literary Criticism

3.6 Evaluate the meaning of archetypal patterns and symbols that are found in myth and tradition by using literature from different eras and cultures.

3.7 Evaluate the author's use of various techniques (e.g., appeal of characters in a picture book, logic and credibility of plots and settings, use of figurative language) to influence readers' perspectives.

Writing Standards

1.0 Writing Strategies

Students write clear, coherent, and focused essays. The writing exhibits the students' awareness of the audience and purpose. Essays contain formal introductions, supporting evidence, and conclusions. Students progress through the stages of the writing process as needed.

Organization and Focus

1.1 Create multiple-paragraph narrative compositions:
   a. Establish and develop a situation or plot.
   b. Describe the setting.
   c. Present an ending.

1.2 Create multiple-paragraph expository compositions:
   a. Establish a topic, important ideas, or events in sequence or chronological order.
   b. Provide details and transitional expressions that link one paragraph to another in a clear line of thought.
   c. Offer a concluding paragraph that summarizes important ideas and details.

Research and Technology

1.3 Use organizational features of printed text (e.g., citations, end notes, bibliographic references) to locate relevant information.

1.4 Create simple documents by using electronic media and employing organizational features (e.g., passwords, entry and pull-down menus, word searches, a thesaurus, spell checks).

1.5 Use a thesaurus to identify alternative word choices and meanings.

Evaluation and Revision

1.6 Edit and revise manuscripts to improve the meaning and focus of writing by adding, deleting, consolidating, clarifying, and rearranging words and sentences.

2.0 Writing Applications (Genres and Their Characteristics)

Students write narrative, expository, persuasive, and descriptive texts of at least 500 to 700 words in each genre. Student writing demonstrates a command of standard American English and the research, organizational, and drafting strategies outlined in Writing Standard 1.0.

Using the writing strategies of grade five outlined in Writing Standard 1.0, students:

2.1 Write narratives:
   a. Establish a plot, point of view, setting, and conflict.
   b. Show, rather than tell, the events of the story.

2.2 Write responses to literature:
   a. Demonstrate an understanding of a literary work.
   b. Support judgments through references to the text and to prior knowledge.
   c. Develop interpretations that exhibit careful reading and understanding.

2.3 Write research reports about important ideas, issues, or events by using the following guidelines:
   a. Frame questions that direct the investigation.
   b. Establish a controlling idea or topic.
   c. Develop the topic with simple facts, details, examples, and explanations.

2.4 Write persuasive letters or compositions:
   a. State a clear position in support of a proposal.
   b. Support a position with relevant evidence.
   c. Follow a simple organizational pattern.
   d. Address reader concerns.

Written and Oral English-Language Conventions Standards

1.0 Written and Oral English Language Conventions

Students write and speak with a command of standard English conventions appropriate to this grade level.

Sentence Structure

1.1 Identify and correctly use prepositional phrases, appositives, and independent and dependent clauses; use transitions and conjunctions to connect ideas.

Grammar

1.2 Identify and correctly use verbs that are often misused (e.g., *lie/lay, sit/set, rise/raise*), modifiers, and pronouns.

Punctuation

1.3 Use a colon to separate hours and minutes and to introduce a list; use quotation marks around the exact words of a speaker and titles of poems, songs, short stories, and so forth.

Capitalization

1.4 Use correct capitalization.

Spelling

1.5 Spell roots, suffixes, prefixes, contractions, and syllable constructions correctly.

Listening and Speaking Standards

1.0 Listening and Speaking Strategies

Students deliver focused, coherent presentations that convey ideas clearly and relate to the background and interests of the audience. They evaluate the content of oral communication.

Comprehension

1.1 Ask questions that seek information not already discussed.

1.2 Interpret a speaker's verbal and nonverbal messages, purposes, and perspectives.

1.3 Make inferences or draw conclusions based on an oral report.

Organization and Delivery of Oral Communication

1.4 Select a focus, organizational structure, and point of view for an oral presentation.

1.5 Clarify and support spoken ideas with evidence and examples.

1.6 Engage the audience with appropriate verbal cues, facial expressions, and gestures.

Analysis and Evaluation of Oral and Media Communications

1.7 Identify, analyze, and critique persuasive techniques (e.g., promises, dares, flattery, glittering generalities); identify logical fallacies used in oral presentations and media messages.

1.8 Analyze media as sources for information, entertainment, persuasion, interpretation of events, and transmission of culture.

2.0 Speaking Applications (Genres and Their Characteristics)

Students deliver well-organized formal presentations employing traditional rhetorical strategies (e.g., narration, exposition, persuasion, description). Student speaking demonstrates a command of Standard American English and the organizational and delivery strategies outlined in Listening and Speaking Standard 1.0.

Using the speaking strategies of grade five outlined in Listening and Speaking Standard 1.0, students:

2.1 Deliver narrative presentations:
   a. Establish a situation, plot, point of view, and setting with descriptive words and phrases.

b. Show, rather than tell, the listener what happens.

c. 2.2 Deliver informative presentations about an important idea, issue, or event by the following means:

    d. Frame questions to direct the investigation.

    e. Establish a controlling idea or topic.

    f. Develop the topic with simple facts, details, examples, and explanations.

2.3 Deliver oral responses to literature:

    a. Summarize significant events and details.

    b. Articulate an understanding of several ideas or images communicated by the literary work.

    c. Use examples or textual evidence from the work to support conclusions.

ENGLISH-LANGUAGE DEVELOPMENT

Reading Standards

Beginning

Word Analysis

B1. Recognize English phonemes that correspond to phonemes students already hear and produce while reading aloud.

B2. Recognize sound/symbol relationships in one's own writing.

Fluency and Systematic Vocabulary Development

B3. Read aloud simple words (e.g., nouns and adjectives) in stories or games.

B4. Respond appropriately to some social and academic interactions (e.g., simple question/answer, negotiate play).

B5. Demonstrate comprehension of simple vocabulary with an appropriate action.

B6. Retell simple stories by using drawings, words, or phrases.

B7. Produce simple vocabulary (single words or short phrases) to communicate basic needs in social and academic settings (e.g., locations, greetings, classroom objects).

Reading Comprehension

B8. Respond orally to stories read aloud by giving one- or two-word responses (e.g., "brown bear") to factual comprehension questions.

B9. Orally identify the relationship between simple text read aloud and one's own experience by using key words and/or phrases.

B10. Understand and follow simple one-step directions for classroom activities.

B11. Identify, using key words or pictures, the basic sequence of events in stories read aloud.

B12. Identify, using key words and/or phrases, the main idea in a story read aloud.

B13. Point out text features, such as the title, table of contents, and chapter headings.

Literary Response and Analysis

B14. Listen to a story and respond orally in one or two words to factual comprehension questions.

B15. Identify orally different characters and settings in simple literary texts by using words or phrases.

B16. Distinguish between fiction and nonfiction by giving one- or two-word oral responses.

B17. Create pictures, lists, charts, and tables to identify the characteristics of fairy tales, folktales, myths, and legends.

Early Intermediate

Word Analysis

EI1. While reading aloud, recognize and produce English phonemes that do not correspond to phonemes students already hear and produce (e.g., *a* in *cat* and final consonants).

EI2. Recognize common English morphemes in phrases and simple sentences (e.g., basic syllabication rules and phonics).

Fluency and Systematic Vocabulary Development

EI3. Apply knowledge of content-related vocabulary to discussions and reading.

EI4. Read simple vocabulary, phrases, and sentences independently.

EI5. Use knowledge of English morphemes, phonics, and syntax to decode and interpret the meaning of unfamiliar words in simple sentences.

EI6. Demonstrate internalization of English grammar, usage, and word choice by recognizing and correcting some errors when speaking or reading aloud.

EI7. Read aloud with some pacing, intonation, and expression one's own writing of narrative and expository texts.

Reading Comprehension

EI8. Read and listen to simple stories and demonstrate understanding by using simple sentences to respond to explicit detailed questions (e.g., "The bear is brown.").

EI9. Read and orally identify relationships between written text and one's own experience by using simple sentences.

EI10. Understand and follow simple two-step directions for classroom activities.

EI11. Orally identify, using simple sentences, the basic sequence of events in text that one reads.

EI12. Read text and orally identify the main ideas by using simple sentences and drawing inferences about the text.

EI13. Read and identify basic text features, such as the title, table of contents, and chapter headings.

EI14. Orally identify examples of fact and opinion in familiar texts read aloud.

Literary Response and Analysis

EI15. Respond orally to factual comprehension questions about brief literary texts by answering in simple sentences.

EI16. Read literary texts and orally identify the main events of the plot by using simple sentences.

EI17. Recite simple poems.

EI18. Describe orally in simple sentences the setting of a literary work.

EI19. Distinguish orally between poetry, drama, and short stories by using simple sentences.

EI20. Describe orally in simple sentences a character in a literary selection according to his or her actions.

Intermediate

Word Analysis

I1. Pronounce most English phonemes correctly while reading aloud.

I2. Use common English morphemes in oral and silent reading.

Fluency and Systematic Vocabulary Development

I3. Create a simple dictionary of frequently used words.

I4. Use knowledge of English morphemes, phonics, and syntax to decode and interpret the meaning of unfamiliar words in text.

I5. Demonstrate internalization of English grammar, usage, and word choice by recognizing and correcting errors when speaking or reading aloud.

I6. Read grade-appropriate narrative and expository texts aloud with appropriate pacing, intonation, and expression.

I7. Use content-related vocabulary in discussions and reading.

I8. Recognize some common root words and affixes when they are attached to known vocabulary (e.g., *speak, speaker*).

Reading Comprehension

I9. Use detailed sentences to respond orally to comprehension questions about text (e.g., "The brown bear lives with his family in the forest").

I10. Read text and identify features, such as the title, table of contents, chapter headings, diagrams, charts, glossaries, and indexes in written texts.

I11. Read text and use detailed sentences to identify orally the main ideas and use them to make predictions and support them with details.

I12. Read and use more detailed sentences to describe orally the relationships between text and one's own experiences.

Literary Response and Analysis

I13. Understand and follow some multiple-step directions for classroom-related activities.

I14. Read literature and content area texts and orally identify examples of fact and opinion and cause and effect.

Literary Response and Analysis

I15. Use expanded vocabulary and descriptive words in paraphrasing oral and written responses to texts.

I16. Apply knowledge of language to derive meaning from literary texts and comprehend them.

Early Advanced

Word Analysis

EA1. Apply knowledge of common English morphemes in oral and silent reading to derive meaning from literature and texts in content areas.

Fluency and Systematic Vocabulary Development

EA2. Use knowledge of English morphemes, phonics, and syntax to decode and interpret the meaning of unfamiliar words.

EA3. Recognize that some words have multiple meanings (e.g., *present/gift, present/time*) in literature and texts in content areas.

EA4. Use some common root words and affixes when they are attached to known vocabulary (e.g., *educate, education*).

EA5. Use a standard dictionary to find the meaning of unknown vocabulary.

EA6. Recognize simple analogies (e.g., "fly like a bird") and metaphors used in literature and texts in content areas.

EA7. Use decoding skills and knowledge of academic and social vocabulary to achieve independent reading.

EA8. Recognize some common idioms (e.g., "scared silly") in discussions and reading.

EA9. Read aloud with appropriate pacing, intonation, and expression increasingly complex narrative and expository texts.

Reading Comprehension

EA10. Describe the main ideas and supporting details of a text.

EA11. Generate and respond to comprehension questions related to the text.

EA12. Describe relationships between the text and one's personal experience.

EA13. Locate text features, such as format, diagrams, charts, glossaries, and indexes, and identify the functions.

EA14. Use the text (such as the ideas presented, illustrations, titles) to draw conclusions and make inferences.

EA15. Distinguish explicit examples of facts, opinions, inference, and cause and effect in texts.

EA16. Identify some significant structural (organizational) patterns in text, such as sequential or chronological order and cause and effect.

Literary Response and Analysis

EA17. Identify and describe figurative language (e.g., similes, metaphors, and personification).

EA18. Distinguish between literary connotations and symbols from culture to culture.

EA19. Read a literary selection and orally identify metaphors and similes.

EA20. Identify the motives of characters in a work of fiction.

EA21. Recognize and describe themes stated directly in a text.

EA22. Read a literary selection and orally identify the speaker or narrator by using simple sentences.

EA23. Read a literary selection and orally identify the main conflict in the plot and its resolution.

EA24. Recognize the difference between the first-person and third-person points of view in a literary text.

Advanced

Word Analysis

A1. Apply knowledge of word relationships, such as roots and affixes, to derive meaning from literature and texts in content areas.

Fluency and Systematic Vocabulary Development

A2. Apply knowledge of common root words and affixes when they are attached to known vocabulary.

A3. Recognize that some words have multiple meanings and apply this knowledge consistently.
A4. Apply knowledge of academic and social vocabulary to achieve independent reading.
A5. Use common idioms, some analogies, and metaphors in discussion and reading.
A6. Use a standard dictionary to determine the meaning of unknown words.
A7. Read aloud with appropriate pacing, intonation, and expression narrative and expository texts.

Reading Comprehension
A8. Use the text (such as the ideas, illustrations, titles) to draw inferences and conclusions and make generalizations.
A9. Describe main ideas and supporting details, including supporting evidence.
A10. Use text features, such as format, diagrams, charts, glossaries, indexes, and the like, to locate and draw information from text.
A11. Identify significant structural (organizational) patterns in text, such as compare and contrast, sequential and chronological order, and cause and effect.
A12. Distinguish fact from opinion and inference and cause from effect in text.

Literary Response and Analysis
A13. Describe the major characteristics of poetry, drama, fiction, and nonfiction.
A14. Identify various techniques to influence readers' perspectives and evaluate the author's use of the techniques.
A15. Recognize and describe themes stated directly or implied in literary texts.
A16. Compare and contrast the motives of characters in a work of fiction.

Writing Standards

Beginning
Writing Strategies
B1. Write the English alphabet legibly.
B2. Label key parts of common objects.
B3. Create simple sentences or phrases with some assistance.
B4. Use models to write short narratives.
B5. During group writing activities, write brief narratives and stories by using a few standard grammatical forms.

Early Intermediate
Writing Strategies
EI1. Write short narrative stories that include elements of setting and characters.
EI2. Write simple sentences and use drawings, pictures, lists, charts, and tables to respond to familiar literature.
EI3. Follow a model given by the teacher to independently write a short paragraph of at least four sentences.
EI4. Write an increasing number of words and simple sentences appropriate for language arts and other content areas (e.g., math, science, history-social science).
EI5. Follow a model to write a friendly letter.

EI6. Produce independent writing that is understood when read but may include inconsistent use of standard grammatical forms.

Intermediate
Writing Strategies
I1. Narrate with some detail a sequence of events.
I2. Produce independent writing that is understood when read but may include inconsistent use of standard grammatical forms.
I3. Begin to use a variety of genres in writing (e.g., expository, narrative, poetry).
I4. Independently create cohesive paragraphs that develop a central idea with consistent use of standard English grammatical forms. (Some rules may not be followed.)
I5. Use more complex vocabulary and sentences appropriate for language arts and other content areas (e.g., math, science, history-social science).
I6. Write a letter independently by using detailed sentences.

Early Advanced
Writing Strategies
EA1. Write a detailed summary of a story.
EA2. Arrange compositions according to simple organizational patterns.
EA3. Independently write simple responses to literature.
EA4. Use complex vocabulary and sentences appropriate for language arts and other content areas (e.g., math, science, social studies).
EA5. Independently write a persuasive letter with relevant evidence.
EA6. Write multiple-paragraph narrative and expository compositions appropriate for content areas, with consistent use of standard grammatical forms.

Advanced
Writing Strategies
A1. Write short narratives that include examples of writing appropriate for language arts and other content areas (e.g., math, science, social studies).
A2. Write a persuasive composition by using standard grammatical forms.
A3. Write narratives that describe the setting, characters, objects, and events.
A4. Write multiple-paragraph narrative and expository compositions by using standard grammatical forms.
A5. Independently use all the steps of the writing process.

Listening and Speaking Standards

Beginning
Strategies and Applications
B1. Begin to speak a few words or sentences by using some English phonemes and rudimentary English grammatical forms (e.g., single words or phrases).
B2. Answer simple questions with one- to two-words responses.
B3. Retell familiar stories and participate in short conversations by using appropriate gestures, expressions, and illustrative objects.
B4. Independently use common social greetings and simple repetitive phrases (e.g., "May I go and play?").

Early Intermediate

Strategies and Applications

EI1. Begin to be understood when speaking, but may have some inconsistent use of standard English grammatical forms and sounds (e.g., plurals, simple past tense, pronouns such as *he* or *she*).

EI2. Ask and answer questions by using phrases or simple sentences.

EI3. Restate and execute multiple-step oral directions.

EI4. Orally identify the main points of simple conversations and stories that are read aloud by using phrases or simple sentences.

EI5. Orally communicate basic needs (e.g., "May I get a drink of water?").

EI6. Recite familiar rhymes, songs, and simple stories.

Intermediate

Strategies and Applications

I1. Ask and answer instructional questions with some supporting elements (e.g., "Is it your turn to go to the computer lab?").

I2. Listen attentively to stories and information and identify important details and concepts by using both verbal and nonverbal responses.

I3. Make oneself understood when speaking by using consistent standard English grammatical forms and sounds; however, some rules may not be followed (e.g., third-person singular, male and female pronouns).

I4. Participate in social conversations with peers and adults on familiar topics by asking and answering questions and soliciting information.

I5. Retell stories and talk about school-related activities by using expanded vocabulary, descriptive words, and paraphrasing.

Early Advanced

Strategies and Applications

EA1. Listen attentively to more complex stories and information on new topics across content areas and identify the main points and supporting details.

EA2. Summarize major ideas and retell stories in greater detail by including the characters, setting, and plot.

EA3. Make oneself understood when speaking by using consistent standard English grammatical forms, sounds, intonation, pitch, and modulation but may make random errors.

EA4. Participate in and initiate more extended social conversations with peers and adults on unfamiliar topics by asking and answering questions and restating and soliciting information.

EA5. Recognize appropriate ways of speaking that vary according to the purpose, audience, and subject matter.

EA6. Ask and answer instructional questions with more extensive supporting elements (e.g., "Which part of the story was the most important?").

EA7. Use simple figurative language and idiomatic expressions (e.g., "It's raining cats and dogs") to communicate ideas to a variety of audiences.

Advanced

Strategies and Applications

A1. Listen attentively to stories and information on topics; identify the main points and supporting details.

A2. Demonstrate an understanding of idiomatic expressions (e.g., "It's pouring outside") by responding to such expressions and using them appropriately.

A3. Negotiate and initiate social conversations by questioning, restating, soliciting information, and paraphrasing the communication of others.

A4. Consistently use appropriate ways of speaking and writing that vary according to the purpose, audience, and subject matter.

A5. Identify the main ideas and points of view and distinguish fact from fiction in broadcast and print media.

A6. Speak clearly and comprehensibly by using standard English grammatical forms, sounds, intonation, pitch, and modulation.

English-Language Conventions

Beginning

English Language Conventions

B6. Use capitalization when writing one's own name and at the beginning of sentences.

B7. Use a period at the end of a sentence and a question mark at the end of a question.

Early Intermediate

English Language Conventions

EI7. Use capitalization to begin sentences and for proper nouns.

EI8. Use a period at the end of a sentence and use some commas appropriately.

EI9. Edit writing for basic conventions (e.g., punctuation, capitalization, and spelling) and make some corrections.

Intermediate

English-Language Conventions

I7. Produce independent writing that may include some inconsistent use of capitalization, periods, and correct spelling.

I8. Use standard word order but may have inconsistent grammatical forms (e.g., subject/verb agreement).

Early Advanced

English Language Conventions

EA7. Produce independent writing with consistent use of correct capitalization, punctuation, and spelling.

EA8. Use standard word order but may have more consistent grammatical forms, including inflections.

EA9. Edit writing to check the basic mechanics of writing (e.g., punctuation, capitalization, and spelling).

Advanced

A6. Use complete sentences and correct word order.

A7. Use correct parts of speech, including correct subject/verb agreement.

A8. Edit writing for punctuation, capitalization, and spelling.

A9. Produce writing that demonstrates a command of the conventions of standard English.

Credits

CALIFORNIA

Illustrations

54 Burgandy Beam; 56 Doron Ben-Ami; 66 Drew-Brook Cormack; 78 Drew-Brook Cormack; 113-114 Donna Berger; 122 Dan Bridy; 123 Dan Bridy; 124 Rebecca Peed; 124 Dan Bridy; 127 Rebecca Peed; 152 Doron Ben-Ami; 153 Doron Ben-Ami; 154 Doron Ben-Ami; 156 Doron Ben-Ami; 170 Shennen Bersani; 173 Shennen Bersani; 174 William Melvin; 206 Shennen Bersani; 208 Shennen Bersani.

Photographs

Every effort has been made to secure permission and provide appropriate credit for photographic material. The publisher deeply regrets any omission and pledges to correct errors called to its attention in subsequent editions.

Unless otherwise acknowledged, all photographs are the property of Pearson Education, Inc.

Photo locators denoted as follows: Top (T), Center (C), Bottom (B), Left (L), Right (R), Background (Bkgd)

18 Ian Shaw/Alamy; 22 Blend/Punchstock, ©Eric Nguyen/Corbis; 24 (TL) Bettmann/Corbis, (CC) David Bowman/Alamy Images, (TL) ©Visions of America, LLC/Alamy, (TL) ©Robert W. Ginn/PhotoEdit, (TL) ©Ron Sanford/Corbis, (TL) ©Reuters/Corbis, (TL) Corbis; 25 (TR) George Hall/Corbis; 29 ©Jupiterimages/Polka dot/Alamy; 30 (CL) Getty Images; (TL) OAR/ERL/National Severe Storms Laboratory (NSSL)/NOAA, (CR) Jupiter Images; 32 (TR) ©Robert Sullivan/Getty Images; 33 (CR) Getty Images; 34 (CR) Eric Gay/AP Images, (BR) Comstock Select/Corbis; 35 (TR) ©SW Productions/Brand X/Corbis, Jim West/Photo Researchers, Inc.; 36 (BL) Getty Images, (CL) Peter Gerdehag/Jupiter Images, (CL) Walter Hodges/Getty Images, (CL) Brad Mitchell/Mira, (C) SuperStock; 37 (TR) Courtesy of Lane County Historical Museum; 38 (C) Getty Images, (CL) Getty Images; 40 (CR) Layne Kennedy/Corbis, (BR) Atlantide Phototravel/Corbis; 41 (TR) Getty Images, (TL) Jonathan Corey/Getty Images; 42 (TL) AP Images, (TL) Alan Thornton/Getty Images; 43 (TR) Kevin Horan/Getty Images; 44 (B) Bob Thomas/Corbis; 46 (BR) Yuri Arcurs/Shutterstock; 47 (TR) Getty Images, ©Vstock/Index Open; 48 (TL) Danita Delimont/Alamy Images, (TL) Klaus Lahnstein/Getty Images/Stone, (C) Library of Congress; 49 (TL) Danita Delimont/Alamy Images, (TR) Klaus Lahnstein/Getty Images/Stone; 50 (T) Facundo/Fotolia, (BR) Harrison Shull/Getty Images; 52 (CR) ©Corbis Premium RF/Alamy, (CL) ©Digital Vision/Alamy; 53 (TR) Bill Bachman/Getty Images, (TR) Getty Images; 54 ©Jeff Greenberg/PhotoEdit; 56 Chad Ehlers/Stock Connection, (TL) RAYMOND GEHMAN/National Geographic Image Collection, (TL) ©John Neubauer/PhotoEdit, (TL) ©Duomo/Corbis, (TL) ©Karen Knauer/Workbook Stock/Jupiter Images, (TL) ©Michael Newman/PhotoEdit, (TL) ©Bill Bachman/Alamy Images; 57 (TR) ©DK Images, (BR) Dave King/©DK Images; 58 (BR) ©Image Source; 59 (CR) Stapleton Collection/Corbis, (CR) The Corcoran Gallery of Art/Corbis; 61 (TR) Doug Benc/Getty Images, (TL) ©Purestock/Alamy; 62 (TL) Laura Ogle/Fotolia, (TL) Bartlesville Examiner-Enterprise, Becky Burch/AP Images, (C) Farwell T. Brown Photographic Archive/Courtesy of the Ames Public Library; 63 (TR) Library of Congress; 64 (TR) Siddharth Darshan Kumar/AP Images; 66 (C) Alain Machet/Alamy Images, (CR) Richard A. Cooke III/Getty Images; 67 (TL) Lowell Georgia/Corbis, (TR) Chris Daniels/Corbis; 68 (TL) LWA-Stephen Welstead/Corbis, (TL) Owen Franken/Corbis; 69 (TR) ©DK Images; 70 (BR) ©Jupiterimages/Creatas/Alamy, (C) Michael Newman/PhotoEdit; 71 David DeLossy/Thinkstock; 72 (CR) F Noronha/Lebrecht Collection; 73 (TR) ©UpperCut Images/Alamy, (TR) Tony Freeman/PhotoEdit; 74 (TL) Joachim Pfaff/zefa/Corbis, (TL) Linda Whitwam/©DK Images, (C) Mimotito/Getty Images; 75 (TR) John Hyde/Mira; 76 (TR) W. Perry Conway/Corbis; 77 (TR) Lynn M. Stone/Nature Picture Library, (TR) Tom Brakefield/Stock Connection; 78 (CR) Cyril Ruoso/JH Editorial/Getty Images, (CL) ©Frank Staub/Index Stock Imager; 79 (TR) Arthur Tilley/Getty Images, (TL) David Frazier/PhotoEdit; 80 (TL) Gary Buss/Getty Images, (TL) Pixtal/Punchstock; 81 (TR) Geoffrey Clements/Corbis, (TR) Steve Shott/©DK Images; 83 (TR) SuperStock; 84 (CL) Getty Images, (CR) Getty Images; 85 (TL) Dario Mitidieri/Getty Images, (TR) Graham Tim/Corbis; 86 ©Image Source Limited; 88 (CR) Wolfgang Deuter/zefa/Corbis, (C) Mary Evans Picture Library, (TL) Getty Images, (CL) Bildarchiv Preussischer Kulturbesitz/Art Resource, NY, (TL) ©Annie Griffiths Belt/Corbis, (TL) ©Bettmann/Corbis, (TL) ©Chad Ehlers/Stock Connection/Jupiter Images; 89 Getty Images, (TR) Dave King/Courtesy of The Science Museum, London/©DK Images; 90 (BC) Douglas Fisher/Alamy Images, (BL) Corbis/Jupiter Images; 92 (CL) Getty Images, (CL) Andrew Geiger/Riser/Getty Images, (CR) ©Royalty-Free/Corbis/Alamy; 93 (TL) ©Tetra Images/Alamy, (TR) Getty Images; 94 (CL) Getty Images, (TL) Carmel Studios/SuperStock; 95 (TR) Jupiter Images, 96 (TR) Paul Sakuma/Associated Press, (BR) Ansel Adams/Ansel Adams Publishing Rights Trust/Corbis, (BR) ©The Ansel Adams Publishing Rights Trust Collection Center for Creative Photography, University of Arizona; 98 (TL) O. Louis Mazzatenta/National Geographic/Getty Images, (CR) Mary Ann McDonald/Corbis, (CL) Picture Contact /Alamy Images;; 99 (TL) ©Cephas Picture Library/Alamy Images, (TR) Michael Durham/Getty Images; 100 (C) Yvaonna Prancil/Fotolia, (CL) Colin Keates/Courtesy of the Natural History Museum, London/©DK Images, (CL) ©Olga Orehkova/Fotolia; 101 (TR) Jon Hughes/Bedrock Studios/©DK Images, (BR) Colin Keates/Courtesy of the Natural History Museum, London/©DK Images; 102 (CR) ©Ron Levine/Getty Images, ©Annie Griffiths Belt/Corbis; 103 Greg Johnston/Danita Delimont, Agent; 104 (TL) Getty Images, (CL) ©Image Source; 105 Jim Channell/©DK Images, (TL) Harry Taylor/Courtesy of the Royal Museum of Scotland, Edinburgh/©DK Images; 106 (TL) Getty Images, (C) Philippe Halsman/©Magnum Photos; 108 Michael Ochs Archives/Corbis; 109 (TR) Bettmann/Corbis; 110 (C) Lynn Goldsmith/Corbis; 111 (TR) ©Roy McMahon/Corbis, (TL) ©DK Images; 112 (CL) SCPhotos/Alamy Images, (TL) Nature Picture Library, (C) ©Universal Pictures/Everett Collection, Inc.; 113 (TR) RKO/The Kobal Collection; 114 Radius Images/Jupiter Images; 117 (TR) Julie Markes/AP Images, (TL) Ernest Bachrach/Getty Images; 118 (C) Getty Images; 120 (TL) USDA, (CL) Getty Images, (BL) Nancy Carter/North Wind Picture Archives, (C) Pictorial Parade/Staff/Hulton Archive/Getty Images, (TL) ©Amos Nachoum/Corbis, (TL) © Galen Rowell/Corbis, (TL) ©Hal Beral/Corbis, (TL) ©David Young-Wolff/PhotoEdit; 121 (TR) ©DK Images; 124 (BL) The Bridgeman Art Library/Getty Images; 125 (TL) Tyler Stableford/Getty Images, (TR) Getty Images; 126 (CL) Andy Crawford/Courtesy of Calcografia Nacional, Madrid/©DK Images, (C) ©Royalty-Free/Corbis (TL) Burgess Blevins/Getty; 127 (TR) Andy Crawford/Courtesy of Calcografia Nacional, Madrid/©DK Images; 128 Matthew Ward/©DK Images; 130 (CR) Doug Mazell/Index Stock Imagery/Jupiter Images; 131 (TL) Bob Peterson/Getty Images, (TR) Pool /Getty Images; 132 (TL) Getty Images; 138 (TL) Francis G. Mayer/Corbis, (CL) ©Elizabeth Crews Photography, (C) Getty Images, iceteastock/Fotolia; 139 (CR) Getty Images; 140 (CR) Dave Nagel/Riser/Getty Images, (BR) ©Purestock/Alamy; 141 Getty Images; 142 (TL) ©DK Images, (TR) ©PhotoAlto/Alamy; 143 (TR) Katrina Brown/Fotolia, (TL) ©Geri Engberg Photography; 144 (TL) The Mariners' Museum/Corbis, (CL) Corbis, (C) Corbis; 145 (TR) Bettmann/Corbis; 146 (TR) Getty Images; 147 Bettmann/Corbis; 148 ©Punchstock; 149 (TL) Superstudio/Getty Images, (TR) ©RubberBall/Alamy; 150 NASA; 151 (CR) Arco Images/Schulte, M./Alamy Images; 152 (TL) Carrot Productions/zefa//Corbis, (TL) Jules Frazier/Photographer's Choice RF/Getty Images, (TL) Blend Images/Jupiter Images, (TL) ©Stephen Frink/Corbis, (TL) ©Macduff Everton/Corbis, (TL) ©Dave G. Houser/Corbis; 154 (TR) Getty Images; 156 (TR) Fotolia; 157 (TL) Juniors Bildarchiv/Alamy Images, Getty Images; 158 (TL) ©Woods Hole Oceanographic Institution, (C) Emory Kristof/National Geographic Image Collection, (TL) ©Michael S. Yamashita/Corbis; 159 (CR) Ralph White/Corbis; 160 (CR) Ralph White/Corbis, (TR) Ralph White/Corbis; 161 (BR) Jim Sugar/Gyo Obata/Corbis; 162 (CR) ©Tom Brakefield/Thinkstock, NASA, (CL) ©Francis Abbott/Nature Picture Library; 163 (TR) Stephen Frink/zefa/Corbis, (TR) Purestock/Jupiter Images; 164 (CR) Corbis, (TL) Getty Images, (TL) ©Anglo-Australian Observatory/DK Images, (CL) NASA, (BL) Stocktrek Images/Getty Images; 165 (TR) Brand X Pictures; 166 (BC) Space Frontiers/Getty Images; 167 (TR) Steve Gorton/Courtesy of the Eurospace Center, Transinne, Belgium/©DK Images; 169 (TL) Space Frontiers/Hulton Archive/Getty Images, (TR) Bettmann/Corbis; 170 (TL) Geoff Dann/©DK Images, (TL) DK Images, (BL) NASA, (C) ©Mehau Kulyk/Photo Researchers, Inc.; 171 (CR) NASA; 172 (TR) KATSUMI KASAHARA/AP Images; 173 (C) ©Demetrio Carrasco/Getty Images; 174 (C) North Wind /North Wind Picture Archives, (TL) Hulton Archive/Getty Images, (BR) ©Bobboz/Shutterstock; 175 (TL) Getty Images, (TR) Sissie Brimberg/Getty Images; 176 (TL) Colin Keates/Courtesy of the Natural History Museum, London/DK Images, (BR) Bettmann/Corbis; 178 (TR) Bettmann/Corbis; 179 (TR) Courtesy of the California History Room, California State Library, Sacramento, California; 180 (BR) Corbis; 181 (TL) Bridgeman Art Library, (TR) North Wind Picture Archives; 182 ©Paul A. Souders/Corbis; 184 (TL) Getty Images, (C) Art Resource, NY, (TL) ©M Stock/Alamy, (TL) ©Karen Kasmauski/Corbis, (TL) ©Justin Kase/Alamy, (TL) Blend Images/Jupiter Images; 185 (TR) Andy Crawford/Getty Images; 186 (CR) Hermann Ayerbe/Getty Images; 187 (CL) Andy Warhol Foundation/Corbis, (CR) The Gallery Collection/Corbis; 188 (CL) Lourens Smak/Alamy Images, (CL) Peter Donaldson/Alamy Images; 189 (TL) Reunion des Musees Nationaux/ Art /Art Resource, NY, (TR) Bernard Gotfryd/Getty Images; 190 (TL) ©ub-foto/Fotolia, (C) Jacques Jangoux/Alamy Images, (B) Pete Turner/Getty Images; 192 (TL) Sue Cunningham/Alamy Images; 193 (TR) Woods Hole Research Center; 194 (BL) ©Ralph Wetmore/Mira, (TR) Martin Harvey/Alamy; 195 (TR) James Randklev/Corbis, (TL) Tom Gamache/ Workbook Stock/Jupiter Images; 196 (TL) ©De Agostini Editore Picture Library, (C) Bridgeman Art Library, (TL) Simon Marcus/Corbis; 197 (TR) Bridgeman Art Library; 198 (CR) Getty Images, (CL) Getty Images; 200 (TR) Kristina Williamson/Getty Images,, (BR) Art Resource, NY; 201 (TL) Terry Vine/ Blend images/Getty Images, (TR) Getty Images; 202 (TL) National Motor Museum/Alamy Images, (TL) SuperStock/Alamy, (CL) Amritaphotos/Alamy Images, (BL) David Lomax/Corbis, (C) INTERFOTO/Alamy Images; 203 (TR) Popperfoto/Alamy Images; 204 (CR) Dennis MacDonald/PhotoEdit, (CR) Alan Keohane/©DK Images, (T) Popperfoto/Alamy Images; 205 (TL) Arthur Morris/Corbis, (TR) Wolfgang Deuter/zefa/Corbis, (BR) Jon Hicks/Corbis; 206 (BR) Ralph White/Corbis, (BL) Ralph White/Corbis; 207 (TR) Mike Brinson/Getty Images, (TL) Erik Von Weber/Getty Images; 208 (TL) Alan Schein Photography/Corbis, (TL) ©Jupiterimages/Comstock Images/Alamy; 209 (TR) DK Images; 211 (TL) Popperfoto/Alamy Images, (TR) Getty Images; 212 (TR) Andy Crawford/Getty Images, (BL) ©Anna Peisl/zefa/Corbis, (BR) Richard Leo Johnson/Beateworks/Corbis; 213 (TL) Getty Images, (TR) ©PhotoAlto/Alamy; 214 picturescolourlibrary/Alamy Images.

A Vocabulary Handbook

Antonyms

An antonym is a word that has the opposite meaning of another word. *Day* is an antonym for *night.*

Smooth

Bumpy

Antonym = Opposite

Strategy for Antonyms

1. Identify the word for which you want to find an antonym.
2. Think of other words or phrases that have the opposite meaning.
3. Use a thesaurus to help you find antonyms.
4. Use a dictionary to check antonyms' meanings so that you use the word that best communicates your ideas.

Synonyms

Synonyms are two or more words that have the same meaning or nearly the same meaning.

Wash

Synonym = Same

Clean

Strategy for Synonyms

1. Identify the word for which you want to find a synonym.
2. Think of other words or phrases that have the same, or almost the same, meaning.
3. Use a thesaurus to help you find more synonyms, and make a list.
4. Use a dictionary to find the word that best communicates your ideas.

Base Words/Root Words

A base word, also called a root word, is a word that can't be broken into smaller words.

Earth

Unearthly

Earth is the base word.

Strategy for Base Words

1. Look for a base word in the unknown word.
2. Determine the meaning of the base word.
3. Guess the meaning of the unfamiliar word. Does it make sense in the sentence?
4. Check your meaning in the dictionary.

Prefixes

A prefix is a word part added onto the front of a base word to form a new word.

Formal

Informal

Strategy for Prefixes

1. Look at the unknown word and identify the prefix.
2. What does the base word mean? If you're not sure, check the dictionary.
3. Use what you know about the base word and the prefix to figure out the meaning of the unknown word.
4. Use the dictionary to check your guess.

Common Prefixes and Their Meanings

un-	not
re-	again, back
in-	not
dis-	not, opposite of
pre-	before

Suffixes

A suffix is a word part added to the end of a base word to form a new word.

Sleeve

Sleeveless

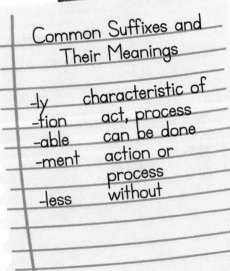

Common Suffixes and Their Meanings

-ly	characteristic of
-tion	act, process
-able	can be done
-ment	action or process
-less	without

Strategy for Suffixes

1. Look at the unknown word and identify the suffix.
2. What does the base word mean? If you're not sure, check a dictionary.
3. Use what you know about the base word and the suffix to figure out the meaning of the unknown word.
4. Use a dictionary to check your guess.

Context Clues

Context clues are the words and sentences found around an unknown word that may help you figure out a word's meaning.

ROARY

BIG BLUE

I saw many animals at the zoo! I saw an elephant, a lion, capybaras, and a monkey.

Strategy for Context Clues

1. Look for clues in the words and phrases around the unknown word.
2. Take a guess at the word's meaning. Does it make sense in the sentence?
3. Use a dictionary to check your guess.

Word Families

Word families are related words that all have the same base word.

Illustrate

Reillustrate

Illustrator

Strategy for Word Families

1. Find the base word in your unknown word.
2. Identify the meaning of the base word.
3. Guess the meaning of the unfamiliar word. Does it make sense in the sentence?
4. Use a dictionary to check your guess.

Word Origins: Roots

Many English words contain Greek and Latin roots.

Automobile

Telescope

Television

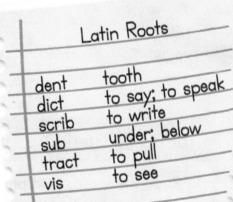

Latin Roots

dent	tooth
dict	to say; to speak
scrib	to write
sub	under; below
tract	to pull
vis	to see

Greek Roots

auto	self
bio	life
micro	very small
ology	the study of
phon	sound; voice
scope	see
tele	far

Strategy for Roots

1. Using what you know about roots, guess the meaning of the unknown word.
2. Does your guess make sense in the sentence?
3. Use a dictionary to check your guess.

W•9

Multiple-Meaning Words

Multiple-meaning words are words that have different meanings depending on how they are used. Homonyms, homographs, and homophones are all multiple-meaning words.

Homographs

Homographs are words that are spelled the same but have different meanings and are sometimes pronounced differently.

Wind

Wind

Some Common Homographs

- bass
- close
- contract
- lead
- live
- present

Strategy for Homographs

1. Read the words and phrases near the homograph.
2. Think about the homograph's different meanings, and decide which one makes the most sense in the sentence.
3. Reread the sentence with your guess to see if it makes sense.
4. Check your guess in a dictionary.

Homonyms

Homonyms are words that are pronounced the same and have the same spelling, but their meanings are different.

Pitcher

Pitcher

Strategy for Homonyms

1. Read the words and phrases near the homonym.
2. Think about the homonym's different meanings, and decide which one makes the most sense.
3. Reread the sentence with your guess to see if it makes sense.
4. Use a dictionary to check your guess.

Some Common Homonyms

pen
duck
mail
ear
bank
bark

Homophones

Homophones are words that are pronounced the same way but have different spellings and meanings.

Eight

Ate

Some Common Homophones

ate	eight
bored	board
brake	break
knight	night
weight	wait

Strategy for Homophones

1. Think about the different spellings and meanings of the homophone.
2. Check a dictionary for the definitions of the words.
3. Use the word that best fits your writing.

Dictionary

A dictionary is a reference book that lists words alphabetically. It can be used to look up definitions, parts of speech, spelling, and other forms of words.

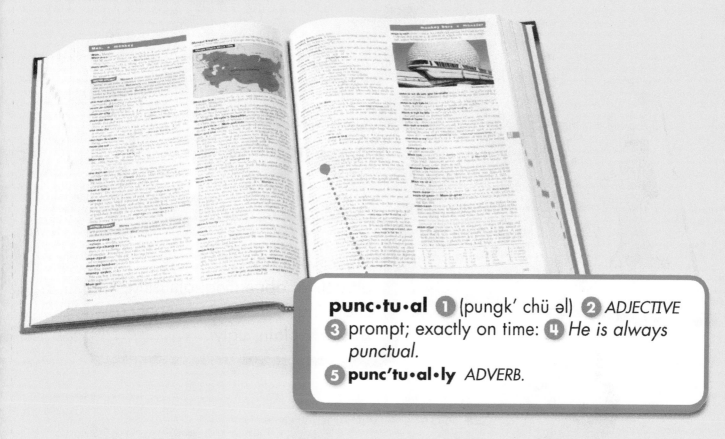

punc·tu·al ❶ (pungk' chü əl) ❷ *ADJECTIVE*
❸ prompt; exactly on time: ❹ *He is always punctual.*
❺ **punc'tu·al·ly** *ADVERB.*

Strategy for Dictionary

1. Identify the unknown word.
2. Look up the word in a dictionary. Entries are listed alphabetically.
3. Find the part of the entry that has the information you are looking for.
4. Use the diagram above as a guide to help you locate the information you want.

❶ Pronunciation

❷ Part of speech

❸ Definitions

❹ Example sentence

❺ Other form of the word and its part of speech

Thesaurus

A thesaurus is a book of synonyms. A thesaurus will also list antonyms for many words.

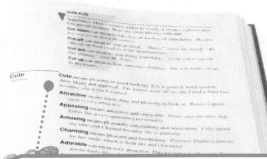

cute
adjective
attractive, appealing, amusing, charming, adorable, enchanting.
ANTONYMS: plain, ugly

Strategy for Thesaurus

1. Look up the word in a thesaurus. Entries are listed alphabetically.
2. Locate the synonyms and any antonyms for your word.
3. Find the word with the exact meaning you want.